THE REFRACTIVE THINKER®

AN ANTHOLOGY OF DOCTORAL WRITERS

VOLUME XII
Cybersecurity
in an Increasingly Insecure World

Edited by Dr. Cheryl A. Lentz

THE REFRACTIVE THINKER® PRESS

The Refractive Thinker®: An Anthology of Higher Learning
Vol XII: Cybersecurity

The Refractive Thinker® Press
www.RefractiveThinker.com
blog: www.DissertationPublishing.com

 Please visit us on Facebook and like our Fan page.
www.facebook.com/refractivethinker

All rights reserved. No part of this book may be reproduced or transmitted in any form or by any means, graphic, electronic or mechanical, including photocopying, recording, taping, Web distribution, or by any informational storage and retrieval system without written permission from the publisher except for the inclusion of brief quotations in a review or scholarly reference.

Books are available through The Refractive Thinker® Press at special discounts for bulk purchases for the purpose of sales promotion, seminar attendance, or educational purposes. Special volumes can be created for specific purposes and to organizational specifications. Please contact us for further details.

Individual authors own the copyright to their individual materials.
The Refractive Thinker® Press has each author's permission to reprint.

Copyright © 2017 by The Refractive Thinker® Press
Managing Editor: Dr. Cheryl A. Lentz • DrCherylLentz@gmail.com

Library of Congress Control Number: 2013945437

Volume ISBNs   Soft Cover   978-0-9974399-2-2
               E-book/PDF   978-0-9974399-3-9
               *Kindle and electronic versions available

Refractive Thinker® logo by Joey Root; The Refractive Thinker® Press logo design by Jacqueline Teng; cover design and production by Gary A. Rosenberg, www.thebookcouple.com.

Printed in the United States of America

10 9 8 7 6 5 4 3 2 1

Contents

Foreword, vii

Preface, xiii

Acknowledgments, xvii

CHAPTER 1
Dr. Tracy Celaya, 1
Cybersecurity in Human Resources on Multiple Fronts

CHAPTER 2
Dr. Joe Hage, 19
Effect of Cybersecurity Risks on Business Continuity and Organizational Performance

CHAPTER 3
Dr. Adam Pierce, 39
Hiring Outsourced Cybersecurity Professionals for DoD Contracts

CHAPTER 4
Dr. Ivan Salaberrios, 55
Using Cryptocurrencies to Fund Small Business: Managing the Cybersecurity Risks

CHAPTER 5
Dr. Loyce Chithambo, 75
Challenges of Setting Policy to Reduce Cyber Attacks in the Information Technology Industry

CHAPTER 6
Dr. James Rice, 97
The Healthcare Cybersecurity Challenge

CHAPTER 7
Dr. Susie Schild & Dr. Robert Boggs, 123
The Cloud and Cybersecurity Threats for the Non-IT Leader

CHAPTER 8
Dr. Temeaka Gray, Dr. Aaron Glassman, Dr. Cheryl Lentz & Dr. Gillian Silver, 141
The Impacts of Integrity and Ethics on Cybersecurity in Higher Education

Index, 167

2017 Catalog, 169

The important thing is not to stop questioning. Curiosity has its own reason for existing. One cannot help but be in awe when he / she contemplates the mysteries of eternity, of life, of the marvelous structure of reality. It is enough if one tries merely to comprehend a little of this mystery every day. Never lose a holy curiosity.

—Albert Einstein

Foreword

The headlines have been screaming for several years about cyber-attacks that hit every aspect of our daily lives. What once was solely the province of credit card fraud has now extended to phishing for personal details. Infections bring malicious code that does everything from destroy your hard disk to steal your personal information to encrypt your files and hold them for ransom to turn your PC or cell phone, or even TV, into a mindless drone in a massive bot army ready to wreak havoc in your digital name. Where does it stop? We can no longer trust the news now that bots push fake news to drive up clicks, we worry about the lights going off because power plants are under siege, and now we wonder if we can trust our elections.

One of the key factors that drove us to write the *CISO Desk Reference Guide* was the realization that we're outmanned and out gunned. Outmanned in that we need thousands more cybersecurity specialists than are available today, and many firms are hiring their first Chief Information Security Officer (CISO). Out gunned in that the tools of the past, that aimed to deploy a firewall to protect a well-defined and completely self-contained enterprise network, are no longer even a meager deterrent for a mildly determined cybercriminal. We can no longer even draw the distinction between cybercrime and nation-state activity, as recent reports acknowledge that the criminals are almost as well equipped as the spies.

What is critically important is that we bring all the soft power and all the hard power we can muster against this threat. We envision a world that is safe from threats and to get there, society must become educated, we must act in unison, and we must become more informed consumers and a more informed electorate. As we engage more in how to make our world safer, we must recognize each person's role and resist the temptation to assume our government or big industry bears sole responsibility. We didn't eradicate most infectious disease in the developed world by leaving it to just the doctors, and we're not going to rid the world of cybercrime and cyber terrorism by leaving it to the experts alone.

It is with this backdrop that Dr. Cheryl Lentz continues her award-winning *The Refractive Thinker®* series by bringing forth doctoral theses on cybersecurity in a new volume XII: *Cybersecurity in an Increasingly Insecure World*. In this pivotal work, her scholars are approaching the cybersecurity issue from all the right angles. Dr. Tracy Celaya and Dr. Adam Pierce look at the challenges of cybersecurity in human resources and getting talent right in *Cybersecurity in Human Resources on Multiple Fronts* and *Hiring Outsourced Cybersecurity Professionals for Government Contracts*, respectively. Several authors address cybersecurity issues in the realm of higher education, where profound changes must be made to bring critical skills to those who are preparing to enter the cyber workforce. These works include addressing integrity and ethics, as well as raising awareness of cybersecurity in the higher education domain, because yes, our schools are under attack as well.

Foreword

These acclaimed authors bring critical thinking to many of the topics so important to the cybersecurity discussion. From setting policy as discussed by Dr. Loyce Chithambo, to using cryptocurrencies as put forth by Dr. Ivan Salaberrios, to understanding the effect of cybersecurity risks on business continuity and organizational performance as explored by Dr. Joe Hage, these topics are timely and the need for scholarly treatment has never been greater.

As you read the pages ahead, we ask you to ask yourself: "What should I be doing to make a safer cyber world?" This is critically important if we're to reap the benefits promised in this new digital age.

About the Authors . . .

Bill Bonney, Matt Stamper, and **Gary Hayslip** met in the summer of 2014 as members of the very inclusive and collaborative cybersecurity community of San Diego, California. Besides being the eighth largest city in the U.S. and a very welcoming community, San Diego is home to several pockets of technological innovation. These include very successful biotechnology, life sciences, and mobile technology industries; a plethora of defense contractors and aerospace research companies; a blossoming startup community in the Internet of Things (IoT) and Cybersecurity; and a thriving academic environment. San Diego is also home to the fewest number of *Fortune 500* company headquarters, per capita, in the United States.

Each of the authors has enjoyed over 30 years of success in the Information Technology (IT) field, but they have very different backgrounds. It became obvious as they got to know each other by participating on panels and speaking at industry events that these different backgrounds brought diverse and complementary perspectives to the problems the cybersecurity community currently faces. What started as a panel discussion on the role of the modern CISO sparked such a lively audience discussion that the authors began to consider turning it into a book for new CISOs and CISOs at mid-size firms in particular. The result is the *CISO Desk Reference Guide, a Practical Guide for CISOs*.

http://www.cisodrg.com

About the Authors...

Bill Bonney, CISA, is a Principal Consulting Analyst at TechVision Research with specialties in information security, Internet of Things (IoT) security and identity management. Prior to joining TechVision Research, he held numerous senior information security roles in various industries, including financial services, software and manufacturing.

Bill is a member of the Board of Advisors for CyberTECH, a San Diego incubator, and in on the board of directors for the San Diego CISO Round Table, a professional group focused on building relationships and fostering collaboration in information security management. Bill is a highly regarded speaker and panelist addressing technology and security concerns. He holds a Bachelor of Science degree in Computer Science and Applied Mathematics from Albany University.

LinkedIn Profile: https://www.linkedin.com/in/billbonney

Matt Stamper, CISA, CIPP-US, brings a multidisciplinary understanding to cybersecurity. His diverse domain knowledge spans IT service management (ITSM), cloud services, control design and assessment (Sarbanes-Oxley, HIPAA/HITECH), privacy, governance, enterprise risk management (ERM), as well as international experience in both Latin America and China. His executive-level experience with managed services, cybersecurity, data centers, networks services, and ITSM provides a unique perspective on the fast-changing world of enterprise IT, IoT, and cloud services.

Matt received a Bachelor of Arts from the University of California at San Diego, where he graduated Cum Laude and with Honors and Distinction in Political Science. His graduate studies include a Master of Arts in Pacific International Affairs from the University of California at San Diego and a Master of Science degree in Telecommunications sponsored by AT&T.

LinkedIn Profile: https://www.linkedin.com/in/stamper

Gary R. Hayslip, CISSP, CISA, Chief Information Security Officer, Webroot Inc. As Chief Information Security Officer (CISO) for Webroot, Gary advises executive leadership on protecting critical information resources and oversees enterprise cybersecurity strategy. As CISO, his mission includes creating a "risk aware" culture that places high value on securing and protecting customer information entrusted to Webroot. Gary is a proven cybersecurity professional, his previous information security roles include multiple CISO, Deputy Director of IT and Senior Network Architect roles for the City of San Diego, the U.S. Navy (Active Duty) and as a U.S. Federal Government employee.

Gary is involved in the cybersecurity and technology start-up communities in San Diego where he is the Co-Chairman for Cybertech, the parent organization that houses the Cyber incubator Cyberhive and the Internet of Things incubator iHive. He also serves as a member of the EvoNexus Selection Committee where he is instrumental in reviewing and mentoring Cybersecurity and Internet of Things startups. Gary holds numerous professional certifications including: CISSP, CISA, and CRISC, and holds a Bachelor of Science in Information Systems Management from University of Maryland University College & Masters in Business Administration from San Diego State University.

LinkedIn Profile: https://www.linkedin.com/in/ghayslip
Twitter: @ghayslip

Preface

Welcome to the award winning Refractive Thinker® Doctoral Anthology Series. We are thrilled to have you join us for the 14th volume in the series (Vol II was published 3 times.), *Vol. XII: Cybersecurity in an Increasingly Insecure World.* Join us as we continue to celebrate the accomplishments of doctoral scholars from around the globe.

Our mission continues to be to get research off the coffee table, out of the Ivory Tower of academia, and into the hands of people who cannot only use, but also benefit from the many insights and wisdom found from doctoral research results. The goal is to continue to bridge the gap from the halls of academia into the halls of the business world. *The Refractive Thinker®* series continues to offer a resource by the many contributing doctoral scholars as they offer their chapter summaries of doctoral research well beyond the boundaries of a traditional textbook. Instead, the goal for this series is to use refractive thinking strategies to push the boundaries beyond conventional wisdom and to explore the paths not yet traveled particularly in this evolving digital age of technology.

As we begin a new year of 2017, this peer-reviewed publication offers readers insights and solutions to various challenges regarding *Cybersecurity*, such as issues within human resources, risks on business continuity and organizational performance, outsourcing cybersecurity professionals for DoD contracts, and using cryptocurrencies to fund small businesses; our hope is that you will find answers regarding effective strategies regarding cybersecurity to help guide your efforts in the boardroom, as well as the work space as part of this special edition Vol XII: *Cybersecurity: In an Increasingly Insecure World* that have come from the research and pens of professional academicians and scholars around the world. The premise is to think not only *outside the box*, but also *beyond the box*, to create new solutions, to ask new questions, to proceed forward on new roads not yet explored or traveled. Our premise is to review academic research in a simple to digest executive summary format to offer new ways for business leaders to think about effective practices for strategies in their business based on what new research has to offer specifically moving forward in an insecure world.

With this volume, we add a new dimension to the series where Dr. Cheryl Lentz, *The Academic Entrepreneur* will conclude each chapter from a business point of view to link this doctoral research to applications for your business.

Remember, not only does *The Refractive Thinker*® series offer a physical book, we offer eBooks (Kindle, Nook, and Adobe eReader), and eChapters (individual chapters by author) that highlight the writings of your favorite Refractive Thinker® scholars, available through our website: www.RefractiveThinker.com, as well as www.Amazon.com. Be sure to also visit our social media to include our Facebook page, Twitter, our YouTube Channel, and our groups on LinkedIN® for further discussions regarding the many ideas presented here.

Preface

We look forward to your continued support and interest of the more than 130 scholars within *The Refractive Thinker*® doctoral community who contributed to this multi award winning anthology series from around the globe. Our mission that began with Volume 1 many years ago is to bring research out of academia for application in the world of business to provide answers to the many questions asked.

Acknowledgments

The foundation of scholarly research embraces the art of asking questions—to validate and affirm, what we do, and why. Through asking the right questions, the right answers are found. Leaders often challenge the status quo, to offer alternatives and new directions, to dare to try something bold and audacious, to try something that has never been tried before. This 14th publication of our beloved 15 time award-winning *The Refractive Thinker*® series required the continued belief in this new publishing model, of a peer-reviewed doctoral anthology, by those willing to continue forward on this voyage.

We are grateful for the help of many who made this collaboration possible. First, let me offer a special thank you to our **Peer Review Board**, to include Dr. Jamie Klein, Dr. Ron Jones, Dr. Judy Fisher-Blando, Dr. Elmer Hall, and myself; and our **Board of Advisors** to include: Brian Jud, Dr. Les Paul, and Dr. Jody Sandwisch.

My gratitude extends with a well-deserved thank you to our production team: Gary Rosenberg, production specialist, and Joey Root, designer of the original Refractive Thinker® logo.

Thank you—we appreciate everyone's contributions to this scholarly collaboration.

Job well done! My best to our continued success!

Dr. Cheryl Lentz
Managing Editor and Chief Refractive Thinker®

CHAPTER 1

Cybersecurity in Human Resources on Multiple Fronts

Dr. Tracy A. Celaya

Human Resources (HR), as a critical business component, is responsible for cyber, information, and data security on multiple fronts including hiring the right people, training and testing security awareness, and partnering with information technology (IT) to preserve the security of data and applications (van Zadelhoff, 2016). HR is often responsible for a broad undertaking of creating and maintaining training for ensuring awareness among employees and contractors and behavior demonstration of a security-minded organizational culture. External and internal cyber-attacks occur more frequently and pose a serious organizational threat while security in the cloud is a serious concern for HR leaders required to manage big data, putting HR at the center of a perfect storm. Although an unconventional approach, HR stands to reinforce cybersecurity through the refractive thinking practices examined in this chapter.

In this chapter, the purpose is to identify how HR professionals can transform technology and cybersecurity for HR on multiple fronts, and provide a review of best practices for moving HR into the cloud and understanding the importance of information security for the second largest source of organizational data, human resources. Finally, a review of the areas of responsibility and vulnerability of cybersecurity within human resources as a strategic business unit and how HR leaders are the forefront of cybersecurity with skill set, experience, and technology knowledge.

Cybersecurity and Information Security for Human Resources

Cybersecurity is a broad term often used subjectively however important to understand how cybersecurity fits in relation to HR. The National Institute of Standards and Technology (NIST) described cybersecurity as the ability to protect and defend the use of cyberspace from cyber-attacks (Kissel, 2013). To distinguish between data security and information security, consider data as a raw subset of electronic information transmitted or received, while information gives meaning to data as a representation of facts, opinions, or other intelligence (Kissel, 2013). According to Kissel (2013) of NIST, information security is, "the protection of information and information systems from unauthorized access, use, disclosure, disruption, modification, or destruction in order to provide confidentiality, integrity, and availability" (p. 94). Kissel's definition continues stating information security is,

Protecting information and information systems from unauthorized access, use, disclosure, disruption, modification, or destruction to provide:

1. Integrity, which means guarding against improper information modification or destruction, and includes ensuring information nonrepudiation and authenticity;

2. Confidentiality, which means preserving authorized restrictions on access and disclosure, including means for

protecting personal privacy and proprietary information; and

3. Availability, which means ensuring timely and reliable access to and use of information (p. 94).

However, Craigen, Diakun-Thibault, and Purse (2014) identified five dominant themes of cybersecurity: a) technological solutions; b) events; c) strategies, processes, and methods; d) human engagement; and d) referent objects (of security). Craigen et al. created a more inclusive definition with these themes. "Cybersecurity is the organization and collection of resources, processes, and structures used to protect cyberspace and cyberspace-enabled systems from occurrences that misalign de jure from de facto property rights" (Craigen et al., 2014, p. 17). Given the latter definition, cybersecurity for HR incorporates using secure hiring practices, hiring the right people for all positions including information security, security awareness training, and assessment, compliance with data security regulations, and protecting information and employees with secure systems/technology specifically, cloud technologies.

Moving HR into the Cloud

Technology continues to evolve faster than business units and organizations can keep up, including the HR function, requiring collaboration between HR and IT to improve HR practices (Stryve Advisors & The RBL Group, 2011). Data security in the cloud drives cloud adoption for large enterprises (Krause, 2016; Staley & Gandi, 2016), while small to large organizations still cite cost as reason to delay moving to cloud solutions and shirk cybersecurity, but still must improve how data and networks are safeguarded. Anti-virus software and firewalls are not nearly enough for consideration as exclusive lines of security in today's virtual ecosystem. Although enterprises are well into maturity on the adoption curve of cloud technologies and services, Cloud-Based Computing adoption continues to slowly increase for other organizations (Celaya, 2015; Computerworld, 2017; Staley & Gandi, 2016). Many companies face technological obsolescence with globalization and high competition (Birasnav, Rangnekar, & Dalpati, 2011), making scalability a desirable organizational goal, and HR leaders indicate a desire for scalability and mobility for global access to data and applications, as leading drivers for modernizing current technology. However, organizations may not be technologically prepared to scale or include mobility as a scalable technology strategy if cyber and information security concerns are not considered and proper security measures incorporated into the solution.

A survey by Stephan, Uzawa, Volini, Walsh, and Yoshida (2016) of Deloitte, found 68% of participants consider HR technology an important to urgent trend. Yet, results from the Sierra-Cedar HR Systems Survey by Harris and Spencer (2016) indicated 42% of surveyed domestic, and more global, organizations have core HR systems located on-site with SaaS solutions consisting of 58%, and Laurano (2014) reported 48% of organizations still manually handle data. Cloud technology is a paradigm shift for distributed applications, platforms, and infrastructures globally accessible through any mobile device with Internet access (Chen et al., 2011). Cloud service providers offer advantages to organizations such as increased collaboration, cost savings, mobility, and scalability (Aljabre, 2012; Carcary, Conway, & Doherty, 2014). Upgrading technology to cloud and mobile can provide HR leaders the opportunity to create a competitive advantage, while addressing security concerns with more network security services offered in the cloud (Krause, 2016).

As cloud technologies are slowly realized, mobile technologies are fast becoming an HR issue (Card & Sivak, 2015) with few organizations currently providing mobile applications for employees. However, mobility with bring-your-own-device (BYOD) and mobile applications is on the rise with accessibility, availability, and mobility of applications and data as leading reasons for implementing Cloud-Based Computing (Celaya, 2015). In Kopochinski's (2016) article, chief information officer, Steve Monoghan stated, data can live anywhere with cloud technologies, making storing, moving, and regulating data far more complex (Kopochinski, 2016). As a result, information security is an increasing focal point for 47% of enterprises (Celaya, 2015; Computerworld, 2017; Sierra-Cedar, 2015; Stephan et al., 2016). More responsibility resides with cloud service providers for offering overall data and cybersecurity for clients whose information resides with them, which may alleviate some HR leader's; however, not at the expense of ignoring the potential risks.

Data privacy is among the leading risks for transferring information through cloud computing (Shilpa & Gopal, 2011). In addition, inconsistent data protection laws, remigration issues when changing service providers, nonexistent disaster recovery by user organizations, insufficient employee training, unauthorized access (Card & Sivak, 2015; Sierra-Cedar, 2015), and lack of control over availability (Aleem & Sprott, 2013) are prominent security risks. Dai, Yang, and Xing (2015) stated security issues, network-transmission problems, and a lack of knowledgeable developers contribute to impediments of cloud technology use with data privacy as an ongoing concern and impediment to cloud adoption (Shilpa & Gopal, 2011).

Celaya (2015) conducted a study of HR professionals regarding the adoption of Cloud-Based Computing in HR. The study used a qualitative research methodology with modified Delphi approach to collect data from HR professional participants to leverage the exploratory technique of subjectivity (Hall, 2009; Skulmoski, Hartman, & Krahn, 2007) using iterative rounds of online surveys. Participants of the study indicated data security and a lack of leadership support among the leading reasons for the slow adoption of cloud technologies. Additionally, Celaya found possible correlations between fear and closemindedness, other priorities ranking higher, and a lack of technology subject knowledge, potentially indicating avoidance of cloud technologies and data security by some HR leaders. Another interesting correlation occurred between scalability and addressing data concerns when implementing cloud technology. The correlation may indicate a decrease in scalability when data security is left an unresolved concern, and be an indicator of an organization's ability to successfully implement cloud technology, particularly when growing. In the study, HR professionals implementing Cloud-Based Computing identified primarily addressing security needs and concerns, including data access, accuracy, and disaster recovery, as among top best practices for successful implementation and adoption (Celaya, 2015). Finally, a correlation emerged between data security, leaders understanding the technology available, and selecting a technology vendor, or cloud solution, with all-in-one integration. The organization remains responsible for ensuring providers offer security in alignment with organizational goals and policies despite more cloud service providers taking on more responsibility for data security, cybersecurity, and secure integration under the information security umbrella. However, secure technology is only part of the issue (Sierra-Cedar, 2016).

The roles and functions of HR continue to change in addition to the use of cloud and mobile technology for HR. Responsibility for human resources as a strategic business unit exists on multiple fronts with data security, training, compliance, and hiring strategy. The migration of HR into the cloud poses challenges for identifying what skillsets HR professionals need (Crane, 2016). Lack of knowledge with the technology available and lack of resources with the right technology skill sets are among the highest challenges to organizations implementing cloud (Celaya, 2015; Staley & Gandi, 2016). Cloud computing may solve many problems companies experience however a talent attainment shortage halts the issues (Drobney, 2013).

Cybersecurity in Hiring

Employees are an organization's biggest asset and its largest threat with information security (Drobny, 2013; Kopochinski, 2016; van Zadelhoff, 2016). On average, only 8% of HR teams have a very good understanding of cybersecurity (Mazor, Schaefer, Tsuchida, Volini, & Walsh, 2016) and are mostly unaware of the security needed for data or the network. IBM's 2015–2016 Cybersecurity Index (IBM Security, 2016) reported people outside of the organization carried out 40% of attacks in 2015 while malicious insiders and inadvertent actors carried out 60% of attacks, putting HR in a key position of responsibility for an organization's information security strategy through the employee lifecycle. Leaders must include security as a point of focus in talent acquisition efforts (van Zadelhoff, 2016). Hiring strategy considerations may include the technology used, recruitment channels, candidate screening providers, and security training for HR professionals.

Drobney (2013) argued cybersecurity is not a technology problem, but a people issue, and an organization's inability to acquire and leverage talent along with the lack of knowledgeable internal resources (Celaya, 2015). The cybersecurity talent gap increases along with the complexity and frequency of cyber threats and reaches deep into all levels of education and generational gaps in the workforce, while some young workers with exceptional potential remain unaware of the information security industry and need for skilled people.

The importance of security must be communicated across business units to place the people, systems, and processes that detect potential threats. Organizational leaders need every employee and contractor with the company to be aware and involved given the ubiquity of technology throughout any organization, large or small, and the complexity of an ever-changing technological landscape (Creese & Upton, 2014). Creese and Upton (2014) suggested adopting a robust internal security policy, raising employee awareness of threat types, critically assessing a candidate's honesty and ethical compass, defining rigorous sub-contracting policies, and monitoring employee technology use. An experienced staff with the skill sets needed for effective cybersecurity is essential and challenging with the shortage of talent. However, closing the talent gap between the cybersecurity workforce and HR professionals aware of digital security, starts with ensuring cybersecurity is an ongoing, enforced, and monitored learning and development directive.

Cybersecurity and Employee Training

Most organizations' security awareness programs are ineffective often enforced annually for compliance or performance management purposes. However, making security awareness a permeating part of organizational culture requires multiple methods of delivery to ensure the message is understood and behavior changed (Dilla, Gal, Raschke, & Steinbart, 2016; Newcombe, 2016). Human error accounted for 95% of security fails consisting of "system misconfiguration, poor patch management, use of default user names and passwords or easy-to-guess passwords, lost laptops or mobile devices, and disclosure of regulation information via use of incorrect email address," according to IBM (2014, p. 3). Human error and malicious conduct can lead to heavy financial and data losses, and become a deterrent for implementing effective technologies for any organization. In a study conducted by Celaya (2015), participants indicated lack of technology awareness and subject knowledge as leading factors impeding organizations from implementing cloud technology, where lack of technology awareness hinders cloud implementation for 36% of HR professionals, directly inhibiting data security.

Organizational leaders must be educated about technology enough to understand the technology available and potential risks in order to make successful business decisions (Kopochinski, 2016). Organizational leaders are among the highest targeted employees of cyber-attacks and must be prepared to consistently practice security awareness and reinforce an information security culture through their actions with support of awareness programs. Awareness programs must educate all employees and contractors on preventative measures from attacks including social engineering.

Social engineering is also known as *human hacking* and is a tactic for gaining access to an employee or consumer's credentials to further obtain access to networks, accounts, and other personally identifiable information (PII) (Conteh & Schmick, 2016). Social engineering attacks consist of phishing, baiting, pretexting, and other tactics (Conteh & Schmick, 2016). Organizational leaders are targeted employees for social hackers attempting to breech an organization's security measures, and must be prepared to consistently practice security awareness and reinforce an information security culture through their actions and support of awareness programs. As such, organizations should promote a culture of security awareness to ensure the safety of systems and data is built-in to organizational culture (IBM Security, 2016). Executive support leads to more widely practiced employee awareness training with emphasis on its importance in cybersecurity strategy.

Implications for Research and Practice

Previous studies by influential research organizations such as Deloitte, Sierra-Cedar, and IBM demonstrated that data security is a challenge and top priority for enterprises, while small to large organizations are slowly realizing security is a top issue. Additional research could prove beneficial investigating security concerns for small to large organizations. Celaya (2015) reported interesting potential correlations with limited statistical significance however significant enough to note and explore further with future research. A final logical direction for future research includes revisiting Celaya's study using a quantitative methodology and a higher number of participants to further validate findings or identify new outcomes from an ever-changing technology landscape.

Conclusion

Organizational leaders expect security to be the biggest leadership challenge between 2016 and 2019 (IDG Enterprise 2017; Hulme, 2015). HR professionals and leaders must understand the complexity of data privacy and security (Mazor, Schaefer, Tsuchida, Volini, & Walsh, 2016). Data concerns include privacy, data integrity and accessibility, internal employee access, lack of disaster recovery measures and service availability (Aleem & Sprott, 2013; Card & Sivak, 2014).

HR and IT develop the infrastructure for technology change and security with people and system resources while influencing readiness and adoption within an organization, making HR leaders core influencers of technology. Top investment drivers included cloud computing and security/risk management by 28% and 23% of IT leaders, respectively (IDG Enterprise, 2017). However, IT Security consists of only 4% to 10% of budgets with competing operational resources dominating the overall budget (Krause, 2016).

Cyber, data, and information security are cross-functional efforts requiring the involvement of everyone from the C-Suite to frontline employees. HR cultivates an organizational culture of information security on multiple fronts; an unconventional tactic, as examined in this chapter. Using a refractive thinking approach, the responsibilities from HR include fortifying an organization's information security strategy with talent acquisition, security awareness campaigns and training, and partnering with IT to ensure the security of data and applications, especially with cloud and mobile technologies.

THOUGHTS FROM THE ACADEMIC ENTREPRENEUR

The problem:
- Identifying how HR reinforces cyber, data, and information security within an organization.

The goal:
- Understanding HR's responsibilities for cyber, data, and information security on multiple fronts.

The questions to ask:
- How is HR currently involved in cyber, data, and information security for the organization?
- What factors must be considered when moving HR systems to the cloud?
- What security features do vendors provide which align with business objectives?
- How do these factors impede the organization's ability to use cloud technologies and ensure a solid information security strategy?
- How prepared is HR to effectively hire cybersecurity staff?
- How technologically inclined are HR professionals to ensure the security of people, systems, and processes?
- Are employees and contractors provided effective security awareness training to encourage behavior change and mitigate the human error factor during cyber-attacks?

Today's Business Application:
- Cyber, data, and information security are among the top concerns for organizational leaders.

- HR leaders who collaborate with IT and senior executives are better equipped to successfully implement cloud and mobile technologies and support the organization's information security strategy.
- Senior executives who support IT and HR in creating an organizational culture of information security are more likely to mitigate cyber-attacks and protect systems, data, and people.
- Security awareness training and campaign effectiveness increases when delivered via multiple channels and supported by senior leaders.

REFERENCES

Aleem, A., & Sprott, C. R. (2013). Let me in the Cloud: Analysis of the benefit and risk assessment of Cloud platform. *Journal of Financial Crime, 20*(1), 6–24. doi:10.1108/13590791311287337

Aljabre, A. (2012). Cloud computing for increased business value. *International Journal of Business and Social Science, 3*(1), 234–239. Retrieved from http://www.ijbssnet.com

Birasnav, M., Rangnekar, S., & Dalpati, A. (2011). Transformational leadership and human capital benefits: The role of knowledge management. *Leadership & Organization Development Journal, 32*(2), 106–126. doi:10.1108/01437731111112962

Carcary, M., Conway, G., & Doherty, E. (2014). Migrating to the cloud. Examining the drivers and barriers to adoption of cloud computing by SMEs in Ireland: An exploratory study. *Journal of Small Business and Enterprise Development, 22*, 512–527. doi:10.1108/JSBED-05-2013-0069

Card, D., & Sivak, M. (2014). *Human resources technology and service delivery trends in 2014: Executive summary research report.* Retrieved from http://hrotoday.com

Celaya, T. A. (2015). *Cloud-based computing and human resource management performance: A Delphi study* (Doctoral dissertation). Retrieved from ProQuest Dissertations & Theses Global. (UMI No. 10004286)

Chen Y., Low, C., & Wu, M. (2011). Understanding the determinants of cloud computing adoption. *Journal of Industrial Management & Data Systems, 111*, 1006–1023. doi:10.1108/02635571111161262

Computerworld. (2016). *Tech forecast 2017.* Retrieved from http://www.computerworld.com/resources/122905/tech-forecast-2017-complete-survey-results

Conteh, N. Y., & Schmick, P. J. (2016). Cybersecurity: risks, vulnerabilities, and countermeasures to prevent social engineering attacks. *International Journal of Advanced Computer Research, 6*(23), 31–38. doi:10.19101/IJACR.2016.623006

Craigen, D., Diakun-Thibault, N., & Purse, R. (2014). Defining cybersecurity. *Technology Innovation Management Review, 4*(10), 13–21. Retrieved from http://timreview.ca/

Crane, P. (2016). SaaS HCM staffing models: Getting out of it what you put into it. *Workforce Solutions Review, 7*(2), 14–17. Retrieved from http://www.ihrimpublications.com/

Creese, S., & Upton, D. M., (2014, September). The danger from within. *Harvard Business Review*. Retrieved from https://hbr.org

Dai, L., Yang, H., & Xing, G. (2015). The construction of human resource management cloud service platform. *Intelligent Information Management, 7*(1), 1–6. doi:10.4236/iim.2015.71001

Dilla, W. N., Gal, G., Raschke, R. L., & Steinbart, P. J. (2016). SECURQUAL: An instrument for evaluating the effectiveness of enterprise information security programs. *Journal of Information Systems, 30*(1), 71–92. doi:10.2308/isys-51257

Drobny, Jr., C. (2013). Cloud computing and cybersecurity are fundamentally HR problems. *World Oil, 234*(12), 26. Retrieved from http://www.worldoil.com/

Hall, E. (2009). The Delphi primer: Doing real-world or academic research using a mixed-method approach. In C. A. Lentz (Ed.), *The refractive thinker: Vol. 2: Research methodology,* (pp. 3–27). Las Vegas, NV: The Refractive Thinker® Press. Retrieved from http://www.RefractiveThinker.com/

Harris, S., & Spencer, E. (2016). 2015–2016 HR systems survey: Innovation, insights, and strategy (18th ed.). Retrieved from http://www.sierra-cedar.com

Hulme, G. V. (2015). Cloud security comes of age. *Forbes, 196*(7), 62–63. Retrieved from http:/www.forbes.com

IBM Global Technology Services. (2014). *IBM security services 2014: Cybersecurity intelligence index*. Retrieved from https://media.scmagazine.com

IBM Security. (2015). IBM 2015 cybersecurity intelligence index. *IBM Security Managed Security Services*. Retrieved from https://www-01.ibm.com

IBM Security. (2016). Reviewing a year of serious data breaches, major attacks, and new vulnerabilities; Analysis of cyber-attack and incident data from IBM's worldwide security services operations. *IBM X-Force Research, 2016 Cybersecurity Intelligence Index*. Retrieved from http://www-01.ibm.com

IDG Enterprise. (2017). *2017 State of the CIO: Executive summary*. Retrieved from http://www.cio.com

Kissel, R. (2013). Glossary of key information security terms. *National Institute of Standards and Technology*. doi:10.6028/NIST.IR.7298r2 Retrieved from http://nvlpubs.nist.gov/nistpubs/ir/2013/NIST.IR.7298r2.pdf

Kopochinski, L. (2016). Scaling down security. *Government Technology, 29*(7), 36–39. Retrieved from http://www.govtech.com

Krause, R. (2016, October 8). Cisco, Palo Alto, Symantec gear up for cloud cybersecurity. *Investors Business Daily*, 1. Retrieved from http://www.investors.com/

Laurano, M. (2014). *Three reasons to move your HR to the cloud. Analyst Insight by Aberdeen Group (white paper)*. Retrieved from http://aberdeen.com/research/8816/ai-cloud-human-resources/content.aspx

Mazor, A., Schaefer, F., Tsuchida, A., Volini, E., & Walsh, B. (2016). HR: Growing momentum toward a new mandate. *Global Human Capital Trends 2016* (pp. 77–84). Deloitte University Press. Retrieved from https://www2.deloitte.com

Newcombe, T. (2016). Erasing human error. *Government Technology, 29*(7), 42–46. Retrieved from http://www.governmenttechnology.co.uk/

Ratheon, (2015). Securing our future: Closing the cybersecurity talent gap. *National Cybersecurity Alliance*. Retrieved from https://staysafeonline.org

Security awareness falls short. (2015). *Information Security, 17*(3), 10–11. Retrieved from https://www.infosecurity-magazine.com/

Sierra-Cedar, (2015). 2014–2015 HR systems survey: HR technologies, deployment, approaches, integration, metrics, and value (17th ed.). Retrieved from http://www.sierra-cedar.com

Shilpa, V., & Gopal, R. (2011). The implications of implementing electronic-human resource management (e-HRM) systems in companies. *Journal of Information Systems and Communication, 2*(1), 10–29. Retrieved from http://www.bioinfopublication.org

Skulmoski, G. J., Hartman, F. T., & Krahn, J. (2007). The Delphi method for graduate research. *Journal of Information Technology Education, 6,* 1–21. Retrieved from http://jite.org

Staley, D., & Gandi, M. (2016). Innovating for tomorrow's workforce: Moving HR application to the cloud. *PwC HR Technology Survey*. Retrieved from http://www.pwc.com

Stephan, M., Uzawa, S., Volini, E., Walsh, B., & Yoshida, R. (2016). Digital HR: Revolution, not evolution. *Global Human Capital Trends 2016,* (pp. 97–103). *Deloitte University Press*. Retrieved from https://www2.deloitte.com/content/dam/Deloitte/global/Documents/HumanCapital/gx-dup-global-human-capital-trends-2016.pdf

Stryve Advisors & The RBL Group. (2011). *Capitalizing on today's technologically talented organization*. Retrieved from http://rblip.s3.amazonaws.com

van Zadelhoff, M. (2016). The biggest cybersecurity threats are inside your company. *Harvard Business Review*. Retrieved from https://hbr.org

About the Author...

Dr. Tracy A. Celaya hails from Phoenix, Arizona. Dr. Tracy is a U.S. Air Force veteran and holds several accredited degrees; a Bachelor of Science in Information Technology (BSIT), a Master of Business Administration (MBA), and a Doctorate of Management and Organizational Leadership (DM). Additionally, she holds certifications as a Professional Project Manager (PMP) and Certified ScrumMaster (CSM). She is affiliated with the Information Systems Security Association (ISSA), Information Systems Audit and Control Association (ISACA), and the Society of Human Resource Management (SHRM).

Dr. Tracy is a Sr. IT Security Project Manager for American Airlines involved in avionics, network, and cybersecurity initiatives. She is President and Principal of Go Consulting International and Chief Operations Officer for a human resources SaaS startup. She also serves on the Fresh Start Women's Auxiliary Board in Arizona.

Her doctoral study, *Cloud-Based Computing and Human Resource Management Performance: A Delphi Study,* included examination of the slow adoption of cloud technology in HR, uncovered best practices for successful implementation, and investigated characteristics of innovative HR leaders successfully deploying Cloud-Based Computing.

To reach Dr. Tracy A. Celaya for information on consulting or doctoral coaching, please e-mail: tracy@startwithgo.com

LinkedIn: www.linkedin.com/in/tracycelaya

Website: www.tracycelaya.com

CHAPTER 2

Effect of Cybersecurity Risks on Business Continuity and Organizational Performance

Dr. Joe Hage

Insanity is doing the same thing over and over again and expecting different results.
—Albert Einstein

Information security is a set of strategies for managing the relationship among people, processes, and technologies necessary to prevent, detect, document, and counter all types of threats to digital and nondigital information assets in all formats whether in storage, in transit, or under processing. Cybersecurity is a fast-changing domain increasing in complexity. Remaining idle and assuming a passive posture are inadequate. Millions of computer and mobile device users are discovering hundreds of millions of vulnerabilities every year; and users around the globe are finding new weaknesses hourly, ready for exploitation. Every day, the media report on several organizations that fall victim to cyber attacks. Oftentimes, such attacks result in the loss of intellectual property, theft of organizational data, and compromise of confidential customer information.

Whenever such intrusions took place, the consequences for the victim organization were grave ranging from fines to lawsuits to diminished reputation to ceasing operations. In fact, cyber criminals have shown an unrelenting ability to breach information technology assets of any organization for extended periods, under the radar. As a result, organizations must evaluate their major cyber risks by implementing information security solutions to counter these rising threats, efficiently and cost-effectively. This paper includes examination of the various cybersecurity risks facing organizations in different industries and discussion of the effect such risks may have on business continuity and organizational performance, with specific mitigation strategies and recommendations. This chapter also features an overview of the Universant information security framework based on the *Assess, Educate, Protect, Comply,* and *Respond* model, a different approach that puts *education* ahead of *protection.*

The Information Landscape

Before delving into how to secure information, exploring the various areas where information resides is very important. Information is not only stored electronically on centralized systems. Information may exist on electronic media, on distributed cloud storage, or in paper format. Individuals may also possess organizational information in different formats. Implementing robust physical security is imperative to restrict and control access of internal employees or external parties to locations where information resides.

In the early 1990s, electronic information was limited mainly to systems inside an organization's four walls. External access consisted almost solely of an e-mail gateway to send and receive electronic mail messages. As a result, organizational leaders focused on securing local area networks and protecting incoming and outgoing e-mail traffic. A decade later, as the Internet became more pervasive, the focus of information technology (IT) staff expanded to protect against incoming viruses and malware intended to target internal servers and workstations.

By 2017, the information landscape became much more complicated, especially with the advent of the Internet of Things (IoT) and Bring Your Own Device (BYOD) strategies. Every device has the ability to send data to and receive data from any other device of any type, anywhere, anytime. Home appliances, cameras, office equipment, cars, trucks, smart homes, electrical equipment, sensors, medical equipment, and other electronic devices transmit trillions of bytes simultaneously around the globe. Startups such as Beebotte Corporation and others are thriving in the IoT space by building and deploying platforms as a service connecting thousands of devices and delivering millions of messages. Such technologies enable developers to build applications that connect anything and everything in real-time.

As BYOD has become a fact of daily life everywhere, employees are bringing their personal electronic gadgets to the workplace and connecting them to the network. Such trends in behavior increase the risks of rogue devices exploring vulnerabilities within the network intentionally or unintentionally. As external and internal threats become intermingled, instituting a solid information security strategy becomes imperative to defend against security threats.

The Cybersecurity Landscape

With information technologies and systems becoming more complex, the infrastructure that sustains them is turning into a more attractive mark. Cyber criminals are infiltrating their targets faster than ever before whereas detecting such breaches is becoming harder than ever (Verizon Enterprise, 2016). According to research, 30% of 1,000 adults surveyed in the United States revealed that they would open a suspicious e-mail message even when they were aware the message contained a virus (Conteh & Schmick, 2016). In 2016, researchers who studied 64,199 cybersecurity incidents found that phishing victims opened 30% of the phishing e-mail messages in their inboxes and 12% of these users actually clicked on the malicious link or attachment resulting in a successful attack, a significant increase over prior years (Verizon Enterprise, 2016).

Ransomware attacks occur when a hacker lures the victim to download a virus that encrypts files on the target computer rendering those files unusable, an action followed by a monetary ransom demand to settle with Bitcoins prior to restoring the files. Bitcoins are the currency of choice for hackers and ransomware cyber criminals. Created in 2009 by an anonymous group of engineers without any governmental regulations, and by design, the Bitcoin currency offers people no possibility to reverse transactions once they are processed (Böhme, Christin, Edelman, & Moore, 2015). Anyone, anywhere in the world has the ability to create a Bitcoin account, free of charge, without disclosing his or her real name, and without undergoing any vetting process.

In 2016, Osterman Research conducted a study of ransomware and related issues by surveying 540 organizations spread among more than 15 industry sectors in the United States, Canada, Germany, and the United Kingdom. According to Osterman Research (2016), the healthcare and financial services industries were the most vulnerable sectors to ransomware attacks. During a 12-month period, 79% of the surveyed organizations experienced some form of a security-related breach of which 39% were ransomware attacks (Osterman Research, 2016).

All business sustainability strategies must address information security risks. Cyber attacks present organization-wide risks that pose significant threats not only to the reputation, but also the mere existence of the affected organization (Rezaee, 2016). In fact, 37% of the 540 organizations surveyed paid the ransom demanded after suffering from a malware infection (Osterman Research, 2016). Moreover, 59% of ransomware entered organizations through e-mail and 24% through website visits affecting 71% of low level staff, 43% of midlevel managers, and 25% of C-level senior executives (Osterman Research, 2016). Traditionally, strategic plans focused on operations, compliance, reputation, and financial risks. However, information security breaches often have a negative impact on operations, compliance, reputation, and finance.

In 2016, research into 64,199 incidents, of which 3,141 were data breaches, showed that financial motivation was behind 95% of cyber attacks with 63% of data breaches resulting from weak, default, or stolen passwords (Verizon Enterprise, 2016). The facilitation of online identity theft is the principal intention for phishing attacks initiated via bulk e-mails and acting as bait to entrap recipients into trusting the sender and divulging sensitive and confidential information (Lötter & Futcher, 2015). A survey of more than 19,000 people from 144 countries found that 97% of the respondents were unable to properly identify the phishing e-mails sent to them (Scheau, Arsene, & Dinca, 2016). Whaling is a type of phishing attacks that targets senior executives in organizations. Cyber criminals prefer going after the *big phish* who may be less technical and may have extensive access to internal systems. Such attack vectors have become well-organized.

Oftentimes, people associate information security breaches with high-tech intrusions. Such assumptions are far from reality because the enablement of cyber attacks is not always high-tech in nature. Some of the common methods to prepare a cyber attack include dumpster diving with someone digging through the target's trash to find sensitive information, social engineering activities to research the target and determine its weakest points, or shoulder surfing with an attacker looking over someone's shoulder to observe and obtain security information (Fan, Lwakatare, & Rong, 2017). In some cases, hackers blackmail employees into helping them penetrate the systems of the organization. Advance fee fraud is another trick that relies on low-tech tricks taking advantage of human greed. In this case, the fraudster contacts the victim via a spam e-mail message with a proposal such as splitting lottery winnings, an amazing business opportunity, or a romantic relationship (Kigerl, 2016). After the cyber criminal hooks the victim, the hacker usually requests advance fees on multiple occasions with nothing delivered in return.

Generally speaking, people must use common sense. If computer users receive a message of any sort that sounds too good to be true, they must ignore it. Why would James, an alleged distant relative of Tom, want to share his inheritance with Tom, whom he never met? Why would a stranger offer Rita millions of dollars in winnings in a lottery she never participated in? Simply stated, no employee should be the weakest link in his or her organization. One must acknowledge that the cyber threat landscape is highly dynamic as cybersecurity experts are constantly improving defensive protections while, in tandem, cyber criminals are becoming increasingly sophisticated. Consequently, cyber risk management must be a continual holistic process touching all stakeholders in the organization.

The Problem

The general problem is that organizations of all sizes in all industries are at the mercy of cyber criminals as they are subjected to distributed denial of service (DDOS) attacks, financial fraud, and theft of organizational resources (Ferdinand, 2015). Large financial institutions face cyber attacks nearly every day (Lemieux, 2015). That being said, one should not assume that technology is the answer to these prevalent problems. Conteh and Schmick (2016) concluded that technology is not enough to reduce the effect of social engineering attacks. Instead, focus must be on people's behavior and human impulses which are at the core of vulnerabilities.

Understanding where information resides is vital to a robust information security strategy. In some cases, the information security and IT personnel are unaware of the existence of certain data silos within the enterprise. In other cases, information security and IT experts do not exert tight control over the information as it changes or as data flow from one system to another. As a result, one cannot protect information effectively at all times if one does not know where the information is stored at any given point in time.

Relentless Cyber Attacks Unleashed

Cyber criminals prefer to target the healthcare industry sector (Kelpsas & Nelson, 2016). In March 2016, a ransomware computer virus paralyzed MedStar Health Incorporated. The attackers targeted hospitals in Maryland and Washington forcing the electronic record systems offline, preventing patients from booking appointments, and leaving staff unable to check e-mail messages or even look up phone numbers. Incoming emergency patients had to be diverted to other hospitals (CBC News, 2016). On February 5, 2016, Hollywood Presbyterian Hospital experienced a ransomware attack. The original ransom demand was $3.4 million; however, the hospital's management negotiated the amount down to $17,000 (Kelpsas & Nelson, 2016).

In 2014, eBay requested more than 145 million of its users around the world to change their passwords because of a security breach. Hackers had accessed user passwords, usernames, addresses, birth dates, phone numbers, and e-mail addresses (Peterson, 2014). Apparently, attackers infiltrated the eBay systems by deceiving some eBay employees to disclose their elevated credentials, through a social engineering attack vector, thus enabling the hackers to breach the eBay systems.

In 2015, major news rocked the financial industry with the disclosure that for 3 years since 2012, JPMorgan Chase suffered a massive hacking attack along with 14 other financial companies. Cyber criminals stole the data of more than 100 million people, making it the largest theft of customer data from U.S. financial institutions in history. JPMorgan Chase clients, 76 million households and 7 million small businesses, constituted 80% of the victims who had personal information stolen such as names, addresses, phone numbers, and e-mail addresses, while other victims included customers of TD Ameritrade and Scottrade (Whitehouse & McCoy, 2015).

In February 2016, the Internal Revenue Service (IRS) uncovered evidence that, several months earlier in May of 2015, cyber hackers infiltrated the IRS systems resulting in the compromise of personal information of more than 100,000 American taxpayers. In August 2015, the IRS disclosed that the data breach was more significant than originally estimated with as many as 610,000 Americans affected. In February 2016, the IRS revealed that more than 700,000

Americans had their personal information stolen (CBS News, 2016).

On September 22, 2016, Yahoo announced that hackers, with the support of a foreign government, stole data from 500 million Yahoo e-mail accounts in late 2014. Stolen information included e-mail addresses, passwords, full user names, and dates of birth, with telephone numbers as well as security questions and answers (Fiegerman, 2016). On December 14, 2016, Yahoo announced the occurrence of another breach in August 2013 that may have compromised the personal information of one billion Yahoo users, making it the largest data breach in history (Yahoo, 2016).

Human Firewalls and Threat Mitigation

In a highly dynamic landscape, defending against all types of cyber attacks is unrealistic (Ferdinand, 2015). Cybersecurity is not a product or service, but a combination of processes, technologies, and people. Humans are often the weakest link in the security chain. The concept of cyber resilience consists of the capability to recover from disruptions and return to stability (Ferdinand, 2015). Thus, building human firewalls is a must and security education, training, and awareness (SETA) are necessary to build organizational cyber resilience.

Cyber resilience must be a key strategic goal for all organizations of any type. Threats to sensitive and private information come in many different forms, e.g. malware, phishing and whaling attacks, identity theft, and ransomware. Ferdinand (2015) noted that "cyber resilience is a prerequisite for continued existence and potential competitive advantage" (p. 188). Organizations must always remain vigilant because their value is proportional to the accuracy and robustness of their information. Hence, securing information assets is not only critical for operations but also to retaining credibility and earning the trust of clients. According to Scott (2015), security threats target industrial control systems because of (a) unintentional infections caused by negligent employees, (b) organized criminals aiming to achieve financial gains, and (c) disgruntled employees. Information security personnel, internally or externally hired, must conduct periodic information security assessments that target people, processes, and technologies using services such as penetration tests, and social engineering exercises. Organizations may be better able to minimize the risks of attacks by bringing people, processes, and technologies to bear. To deter attackers and mitigate vulnerabilities at various points, information security staff must implement and coordinate multiple security controls as part of an in-depth layered defense strategy across the extended enterprise.

Preparedness is most important to maintain the confidentiality, integrity, and availability (CIA) triad of organizational information technology systems:

- *Confidentiality* is the goal of ensuring that sensitive information is only disclosed to authorized parties

- *Integrity* is about preventing the unauthorized addition and modification of data

- *Availability* is to guarantee that only authorized parties can access information when and where needed

Assess, Educate, Protect, Comply, and Respond

Universant Technology Corporation (2017), a cybersecurity firm, has built its information security framework on the

Assess, Educate, Protect, Comply, and *Respond* model. The first four pillars are rooted in preparedness:

Assess is the first logical step to evaluate the current situation within the organization by performing various information security services that target people, processes, and technologies including vulnerability assessments, penetration tests, social engineering tests, secure system and network architecture design, and secure code reviews. Assessing vulnerabilities within the entire organization helps pinpoint existing security flaws. Such activities enable organizational leaders to determine the extent to which systems are compromised before an actual attack occurs.

Educate is the stage focused on promoting information security awareness across the organization using a comprehensive Information Security Education, Training, and Awareness (SETA) program. On the technical side, software developers attend training sessions to learn about writing secure code. Even executive level employees participate in the SETA program because they are primary targets of cyber criminals.

Protect is the phase when IT and information security personnel acquire the ability to manage information security through the deployment of specific processes and solutions that constitute the security management system. The specialists deploy proactive threat management solutions to perform threat monitoring and detection; threat analysis, evaluation and alerting; threat prevention; virtual patching; risk assessment and risk treatment plan. Vulnerability management systems consist of vital capabilities such as vulnerability scanning, monitoring and detection; vulnerability analysis, evaluation, and alerting; vulnerability fixing and patching; vulnerability workarounds; and vulnerability transfer and escalation. Incident monitoring and management activities include event monitoring; incident detection, analysis, evaluation, and alerting; incident remediation; and incident transfer and escalation. IT security system management includes initial system onboarding; ongoing system operation and maintenance; emergency system updating; and technical security policy review and management. Finally, the reporting, review and audit of information security information include data collection and review; threat, vulnerability, incident, and key performance indicators (KPI) reporting; process effectiveness, review, audit and improvement; and performance reviews and audits.

Comply is the step whereby information security experts conduct an information security gap analysis. These experts provide a comprehensive examination and detailed comparison of the existing security program versus the best overall security practices and standards. Typical required standards include ISO 27001:2013 for Information Security Management Systems (ISMS), ISO 27799:2016 for ISMS in Healthcare, the Health Insurance Portability and Accountability Act of 1996 (HIPAA), and the Payment Card Industry Data Security Standard (PCI DSS). Basing an information security program and strategy on international best practices is helpful to the organization, even when compliance is not mandated by laws and regulations.

Respond is the final stage when information security experts and IT personnel respond to security incidents and breaches; and on occasion, they would conduct digital forensic investigations. The designated specialists would perform disaster recovery and business continuity activities to restore normal operations. Digital forensics are an important element to combat cyber crimes enabling investigators to extract evidence from storage media and electronic devices (Waziri, Okongwu, Isah, Adebayo, & Abdulhamid, 2013). Most organizations lack the resources and skills to conduct digital forensic investigations internally. Such activities require expertise and a variety of tools. Consequently, organizations must rely on managed security service providers who have such capabilities as a core competency. Hacktivists, cyberwarfare armies, and cyber criminals are pursuing targets to commit (a) theft of intellectual property, (b) damage of company networks, (c) financial fraud, (d) hacker system penetration, and (e) distribution of execution viruses and worms (Waziri et al., 2013).

Along with preparedness, vigilance starts with the establishment of a risk management program to continuously assess vulnerabilities and threats to information assets and to determine and apply the appropriate protective controls. Organizations must institute an incident response plan (IRP) to prepare for any eventual security breach and to minimize the effect of cyber attacks. Organizations must establish, develop, and test procedures for disaster recovery and business continuity. The relevant parties shall eventually address and fix any security gaps discovered during these tests.

For organizations of any size, investing in training and educating their human resources are as critical as the financial investments made to update and sustain their capital equipment. With repetitive communications and frequent training sessions, employees became better skilled to detect and avoid the lure of social engineering attacks (Conteh & Schmick, 2016). Clearly, an organization's human capital is a key enabler of solid cyber resilience. The employees are the first line of defense for building human firewalls in the fight against cyber crimes.

Cybersecurity Insurance

Cyber crimes are extremely costly to organizations. Following the 2012 breach that affected more than 260,000 clients, TD Bank paid $1.475 Billion in penalties (Lemieux, 2015). Such significant losses may result in destroying the affected organization. Accordingly, cybersecurity insurance may be necessary despite adding to the cost of conducting business.

Marchetti (2015) discussed several options available to organizations to cover losses related to technology breaches as part of an existing business owner's policy (BOP), property insurance, crime and sabotage, errors and omissions, and directors and officers (D & O) liability insurance. Specific insurance coverages include Targeted Hacker Attack / Electronic Vandalism, Interruption of Computer Operations, Employee Dishonesty/Computer Fraud, Privacy Injury Liability, Network Security Liability, Privacy Regulation Proceeding Coverage, Privacy Event Expense Reimbursement, and Extortion Demand Reimbursement (Marchetti, 2015). Managing cyber risks is not as simple as assessing the risks, implementing some changes, and ending the process; thus, periodic audits, assessments, and monitoring are essential for continued compliance (Cascardo, 2016). Risk management is the primary purpose of such policies intended to reduce risks to business and operational continuity, and to cover costs resulting from the willful corruption, distortion, deletion, damage, or destruction of electronic data caused by a targeted hacker attack.

Conclusion

In all likelihood, only two different types of organizations exist in the world: those that cyber attackers have breached and know it, and those that cyber attackers have penetrated and do not realize it yet. Therefore, prevention is insufficient and organizations must invest in detection because their information security personnel would want to know what system breach occurred as fast as humanly possible so that the experts respond and remediate the vulnerability. A successful program of actions is risky and costly—but such issues are less significant than the long-range cost of comfortable inaction. Proactive information security is achievable by using several strategies simultaneously to improve organizational resilience.

Finally, the Universant Technology information security framework of *Assess, Educate, Protect, Comply,* and *Respond* is an illustration of refractive thinking. Traditionally, information security experts tend to assess vulnerabilities in an organization then proceed to execute the resulting corrective actions. The implementation phase would usually include training and education. However, the Universant Technology framework crosses traditional boundaries and challenges the conventional wisdom by placing *education* immediately after the *assessment* phase. The premise is that educating the organizational stakeholders on the findings and potential effects of the assessment phase, and informing these individuals about the likely corrective actions are most important to a successful *protection* phase. In all likelihood, the information security education, training, and awareness (SETA) activities may help align all levels of the organization behind a unified strategy for the information security program. Without executive sponsorship and cross-departmental buy-in, even the greatest information security strategies and plans would be worthless.

THOUGHTS FROM THE ACADEMIC ENTREPRENEUR

The problem to be solved:
- Facing cybersecurity risks that threaten business continuity and organizational performance.

The goal:
- Understanding how to prepare for and mitigate cybersecurity risks to improve the cyber resilience of the organization.

The questions to ask:
- How can organizational leaders prepare effectively to face cyber threats?
- Are any types of organizations or industry sectors immune from cyber attacks?

Today's Business Application:
- Preparedness, vigilance, and human firewalls help prevent or lessen the effects of information security breaches.
- Continuous communication inside and outside the organization tend to help leaders and crisis management teams resolve the crisis and lessen post-crisis effects.
- The Universant *Assess, Educate, Protect, Comply,* and *Respond* model enables organizational stakeholders to set priorities for people, processes, and technologies that are fundamental to improving the information security posture of the organization.

REFERENCES

Böhme, R., Christin, N., Edelman, B., & Moore, T. (2015). Bitcoin: Economics, technology, and governance. *The Journal of Economic Perspectives, 29*(2), 213–238. doi:10.1257/jep.29.2.213

Broadhurst, R., Grabosky, P., Alazab, M., & Chon, S. (2014). Organizations and cyber-crime: An analysis of the nature of groups engaged in cyber-crime. *International Journal of Cyber Criminology, 8*(1), 1–20. Retrieved from http://www.cybercrimejournal.com

Cascardo, D. (2016). Insights into cyber security risks: The key to survival is resiliency. *The Journal of Medical Practice Management: MPM, 32*(3), 169–172. Retrieved from https://www.greenbranch.com/store/index.cfm/product/4_31/the-journal-of-medical-practice-management.cfm

CBC News. (2016). FBI probing virus behind outage at Medstar Health facilities. *Technology & Science.* Retrieved from http://www.cbc.ca/news/technology/mestar-health-facility-fbi-ransomware-1.3509838

CBS News. (2016). *IRS: Computer breach bigger than first thought.* Retrieved from http://www.cbsnews.com/news/irs-hackers-stolen-taxpayer-information-breach/

Conteh, N. Y., & Schmick, P. J. (2016). Cybersecurity: Risks, vulnerabilities, and countermeasures to prevent social engineering attacks. [Article]. *International Journal of Advanced Computer Research, 6*(23), 31–38. doi:10.19101/ijacr.2016.623006

Fan, W., Lwakatare, K., & Rong, R. (2017). Social engineering: I-E based model of human weakness for attack and defense Investigations. *International Journal of Computer Network and Information Security, 9*(1). doi:10.5815/ijcnis.2017.01.01

Ferdinand, J. (2015). Building organizational cyber resilience: A strategic knowledge-based view of cyber security management. [Article]. *Journal of Business Continuity & Emergency Planning, 9*(2), 185–195. Retrieved from https://www.henrystewartpublications.com/jbcep

Fiegerman, S. (2016). *Yahoo says 500 million accounts stolen.* Retrieved from http://money.cnn.com/2016/09/22/technology/yahoo-data-breach/

Kelpsas, B., & Nelson, A. (2016). Ransomware in hospitals: What providers will inevitably face when attacked. *The Journal of Medical Practice Management: MPM, 32*(1), 67–70. Retrieved from https://www.greenbranch.com/store/index.cfm/product/4_31/the-journal-of-medical-practice-management.cfm

Kigerl, A. (2016). Cyber crime nation typologies: K-means clustering of countries based on cyber crime rates. *International Journal of Cyber Criminology, 10*(2), 147–169. doi:10.5281/zenodo.163399

Lemieux, M. (2015). Cyber crime, governance and liabilities in the banking and payment industries. *Banking & Finance Law Review, 31*(1), 113–140. Retrieved from http://www.carswell.com/product-detail/banking-and-finance-law-review/

Lötter, A., & Futcher, L. (2015). A framework to assist email users in the identification of phishing attacks. *Information and Computer Security, 23,* 370–381. doi:10.1108/ICS-10-2014-0070

Marchetti, T. (2015, July-September 2015). Avoid catastrophe by addressing cyber risk. *Nonprofit World, 33,* 10–11. Retrieved from https://www.snpo.org/publications/articles.php

Osterman Research. (2016). *Understanding the depth of the global ransomware problem: An Osterman Research survey report.* Washington, DC: Osterman Research. Retrieved from https://www.ostermanresearch.com/

Peterson, A. (2014). *eBay asks 145 million users to change passwords after data breach.* Retrieved from https://www.washingtonpost.com/news/the-switch/wp/2014/05/21/ebay-asks-145-million-users-to-change-passwords-after-data-breach/

Rezaee, Z. (2016). Business sustainability research: A theoretical and integrated perspective. *Journal of Accounting Literature, 36,* 48–64. doi:10.1016/j.acclit.2016.05.003

Scheau, M. C., Arsene, A. L., & Dinca, G. (2016). Phishing and e-commerce: An information security management problem. [Article]. *Journal of Defense Resources Management, 7*(1), 129–140. Retrieved from http://journal.dresmara.ro/

Scott, J. (2015). Shutdown!: What would that do to your production and profit margins? [Article]. *Loss Prevention Bulletin* (242), 9–11. Retrieved from http://www.icheme.org/lpb

Universant Technology Corporation. (2017). *Information security.* Retrieved from https://www.universant.com/Information-Security.aspx

Verizon Enterprise. (2016). *Verizon data breach investigations report.* Retrieved from http://www.verizonenterprise.com/verizon-insights-lab/dbir/2016/

Waziri, V. O., Okongwu, N. O., Isah, A., Adebayo, O. S., & Abdulhamid, S. I. M. (2013). Cyber crimes analysis based on open source digital forensics tools. *International Journal of Computer Science and Information Security, 11*(1), 30–43. Retrieved from https://sites.google.com/site/ijcsis/vol-11-no-1-jan-2013

Whitehouse, K., & McCoy, K. (2015). *JPMorgan hackers hit Boston mutual fund and 13 other firms.* Retrieved from http://www.usatoday.com/story/money/2015/11/10/alleged-jpmorgan-hackers-named-part-widespread-scheme/75509546/

Yahoo. (2016). *Yahoo Security Notice December 14, 2016.* Retrieved from https://help.yahoo.com/kb/SLN27925.html

About the Author...

Dr. Joe Hage holds a doctorate degree Summa Cum Laude in Business Administration from University of Phoenix, an M.B.A. Summa Cum Laude from Santa Clara University, and a B.S. in Electrical and Computer Engineering from Northeastern University.

Dr. Joe's career spans more than 35 years in operations, administration, finance, information technology, and management consulting. He has a global acumen having worked in the United States and international markets.

Dr. Joe is Chief Executive Officer of Universant Technology Corporation, a provider of information technology and information security solutions. He is also a management consultant with the UNESCO Iraq Office. Preceding this role, he was Associate Chief Information Officer at the American University of Beirut (AUB), a venture partner at PacRim Venture Partners in Silicon Valley, and Chief Executive Officer of eSharing Corporation. Dr. Joe spent 9 years at Agile Software product lifecycle management and supply chain management solutions (acquired by Oracle) where he was Senior Vice President and General Manager, Small and Medium Enterprise Solutions Division (2003–2006), Senior Vice President, Products and Technology (2001–2003), and Vice President, Corporate Marketing (1997–2000). Dr. Joe also held positions at Starfish Software (acquired by Motorola), Novell, Borland, Prime Computer, Data General, and Honeywell. Dr. Joe is a Certified Information Systems Auditor (CISA) and a certified ISO Auditor.

To reach Dr. Joe Hage, please contact: Website: www.joe.me, E-mail: dr@joe.me

About the Company...

Universant Technology Corporation is a leading provider of business-ready enterprise and mobile information technology solutions, information security and cybersecurity solutions, and operations consulting services. Universant provides clients with software development and staff augmentation services, turnkey project execution and outsourced professional services, as well as scalable Web applications and hosting services. Universant delivers information security solutions and services aimed at protecting organizational and personal information. Universant offers operations consulting and business process re-engineering services to help customers improve operational efficiency and their bottom line. Universant's customers are in the technology, healthcare, education, government, banking, finance, automotive, manufacturing, and insurance industry sectors. Universant serves more than 100 global clients with operations in Europe, North America, and the Middle East.

To reach Universant Technology Corporation:
Website: https://www.universant.com
E-mail: info@universant.com
Twitter: http://twitter.com/UniversantTech
LinkedIn: http://linkedin.com/company/universant
Facebook: http://facebook.com/Universant.Technology

CHAPTER 3

Hiring Outsourced Cybersecurity Professionals for DoD Contracts

Dr. Adam Pierce

Cybersecurity is an important facet of daily operations for governments and private companies (Yixin, 2011). Similar to other organizations, the U.S. Department of Defense (DoD) requires a well-trained cybersecurity workforce to complete the nation's cybersecurity mission (Burley, Eisenberg, & Goodman, 2014). The Bureau of Labor projected a need for nearly 100,000 information security analysts by the year 2024 (Bureau of Labor [BLS], 2016). Although a need exists for more cybersecurity professionals, the United States has a deficit of cybersecurity personnel across all industries (Suby & Dickson, 2015). In the state of Virginia in particular, 30,000 cybersecurity related positions remain unfilled (Day, 2014). The DoD has a unique opportunity to enhance the methods associated with hiring cybersecurity professionals. Understanding the strategies used to hire cybersecurity professionals may help to close the hiring gap which is the focus of this chapter. Refractive thinking may help the DoD develop a cybersecurity workforce with the required knowledge, skills and attributes necessary to build and sustain an effective cybersecurity program within the DoD.

The specific problem explored during this research was the lack of understanding of the strategies used by the hiring managers of contracting companies that provide cybersecurity services to the DoD. The purpose of this research was to explore strategies hiring managers used to successfully hire cybersecurity professionals for DoD contracts. A purposeful sample of eight hiring managers with experience hiring cybersecurity professionals for DoD contracts were the participants. Data was collected through face-to-face interviews and a review of job postings for the companies represented by the participants. The data analysis yielded two themes that contributed to the successful hire of cybersecurity professionals; maintaining contractual requirements and strong recruiting (Pierce, 2016).

A scholar-practitioner's goal is not to develop new theories, but to apply existing theories to help find solutions to current problems. For this problem, the conceptual framework used was the organizational learning theory by Argyris (1976). The root of the organizational learning theory is the idea that organizations can increase the efficiency of their processes by evaluating and improving processes using positive and negative feedback (Argyris, 1976). Learning materializes when the process owners observe the results of the process against the intent for the first time (Argyris, 1996). If the lessons learned prove to be valuable, then the organization can augment the current process to include the new information (Argyris, 1976). Hiring new employees is a repetitive process, and evaluating the process after each iteration allows process owners to learn from the successes and failures during the process incorporating the organizational learning theory as the interpretive lens to review findings.

The information found in this paper adds to the current knowledge concerning hiring practices for contracting companies that currently or plan to compete for contracts that provide cybersecurity services to the DoD. An assumption made during the research was the question *Is DoD asking for the proper workforce when writing cybersecurity contracts?* The concern was what if the DoD decided to transition from contracting cybersecurity professionals and started building a cybersecurity workforce with training tailored to the unique mission of the DoD, and how this might impact the industry.

Background of Cybersecurity Landscape

Cybersecurity is unique because of involving aspects of information technology and traditional security. The profession grew in importance as businesses realized the need to protect data and systems from unauthorized access (Dunn Cavelty, 2014). The concept of cybersecurity is to protect information from internal and external threats, while maintaining the ability to use the information system to conduct the organization's day-to-day operations (von Solms & van Niekerk, 2013). Information assurance is the part of cybersecurity with the goal of protecting the availability, confidentiality, and integrity of the organization's information systems and more importantly, the data stored on their information systems (Drtil, 2013; Kumar & Singh, 2012). Striking the perfect balance between security and functionality is a challenge, but achieving the goal is possible when the organization has the right personnel with the right training and motivation.

Developing an information security policy is one way for organizations to enhance the security posture (Ifinedo, 2014). The policy should align with the type of information systems the organization utilizes for operations. The organization's information security policy should also align with the purpose and functionality of the systems (Nielsen, 2012). Without the proper alignment, the organization may create a situation where gaps exist in the organization's security. The exposure can lead to data loss or damage if attackers exploit the security gap (Dunn Cavelty, 2014). A strong, consistently enforced security policy can ultimately increase the organization's security.

Hiring Outsourced Cybersecurity Professionals for DoD Contracts

Theme 1: Maintaining Contractual Requirements

Contractual requirements. The baseline for the hiring process of cybersecurity professionals for DoD contracts are the contractual requirements in the request for proposal (RFP) (Pierce, 2016). The RFP is the process the DoD uses to solicit bids from contracting companies for goods or services DoD desires to purchase (Goldman, Rocholl, & So, 2013). The participants in the Pierce (2016) study agreed unanimously that the first consideration when executing a contract is understanding what the government is asking for in the contract. The requirements included a college degree, industry certifications, and experience in cybersecurity. Having certifications is a requirement found in each job posting listed for organizations represented in the study. A college degree was a requirement for 93% of the organizations in the study (Pierce, 2016). The hiring managers did not mention if DoD organizations typically included a need for the right mix of education, certifications, and experience; the only concern for the DoD was executing the services in the contract (Pierce, 2016). The participants also failed to mention experience as a requirement; however, all of the job postings stated a specific amount of experience required for the position (Pierce, 2016).

Over qualification. Over qualification was a concern mentioned by half of the participants as something hiring managers should consider during the hiring process (Pierce, 2016). Cybersecurity professionals who do not meet the basic requirements do not advance to the interview process. Hiring someone without the qualifications automatically puts the organization in conflict with adhering to the contractual requirements. Over qualified professionals present a different problem. Hiring managers were reluctant to hire candidates who are over qualified, because the over qualified candidate was more likely to leave the contract early if they were able to find similar work with more pay (Pierce, 2016).

Certification and training requirements. Stated and unstated contract requirements for cybersecurity professionals exist within cybersecurity contracts (Pierce, 2016). Some of the stated requirements include U.S. government-mandated courses such as user awareness and operational security training (Turk, 2013). Hiring managers expect the new employees to complete the training in a timely fashion to adhere to the contract and to help maintain the organization's reputation (Pierce, 2016). Additionally, unstated requirements that hiring managers must manage exist. Cybersecurity certifications require continuing education and maintenance fees. The continuing education requirements depend on the certification, but most of the certifications require a range of 20–120 hours of training over a 3-year period (International Information Systems Security Certification Consortium [ISC 2], 2016; Turk, 2013). Cybersecurity professionals must adhere to the requirements of the certification organization to keep the certification current. If the certifications expire, then the employee does not comply with the requirements of the contract. The hiring manager must provide the resources to retrain the employee or hire another cybersecurity professional with current certifications.

Theme 2: Strong Hiring Process

The second theme from the Pierce (2016) research includes a strong hiring process. This theme indicated techniques that make the hiring process better for the organization and better for the candidate. In addition, the theme included information about what organizations should avoid during the hiring process. Understanding how to streamline the hiring process could help organizations when hiring cybersecurity professionals for DoD cybersecurity contracts.

Third-party involvement. Recruiting is an important part of the hiring process (Strohmeier, 2013). The use of third-party can enhance the hiring process (Johnson, Robson, & Wilks, 2014). Matching the skills of the candidate to the position is an important consideration when hiring cybersecurity professionals. The organizations that the participants represented believe using third-party recruiters is a critical part of their success for finding and recruiting quality cybersecurity professionals with the qualifications necessary to fill the contract positions (Pierce, 2016). The organizations that use third-party recruiters were the larger organizations in the group (Pierce, 2016). The smaller contracting companies did not have the funding necessary to support hiring a third-party recruiter to help during the recruitment phase of the hiring process. Over time, the larger organizations learned third party recruiters are a valuable asset, so much so they have institutionalized the use of the third-party recruiters in the hiring process (Pierce, 2016)

Strengths and weaknesses in hiring process. The majority, 75%, of the study participants mentioned the third party human resources (HR) departments, as well as their individual HR departments as major strengths in the hiring process (Pierce, 2016). The participants also mentioned the internal processes of the organizations as a strength (Pierce, 2016). Although the HR department is strength, areas for improvement exist. The first area for improvement is the communication between the hiring manager and the HR department. After the candidate accepts employment, 62% of HR departments represented in the study slow the process for the candidate. The hiring managers want the new employees to start working as soon as possible, because the company cannot bill for the work until the new employee starts (Pierce, 2016). The U.S. government also slows the process because of the requirements they have such as base access, building access, and desktop access (Pierce, 2016). The organization does not have the power to influence the government's processes, but the hiring managers and the HR departments can fix the organization's processes after hire.

The results of the study indicated understanding the contractual requirements and instituting a strong recruitment process provide a competitive advantage to organizations the hire cybersecurity professionals for DoD contracts. The study also posited that the use of organizational learning enhances the processes involved in hiring cybersecurity professionals for DoD contracts (Pearce, 2016). The research adds to the current literature in human resources (HR) and cybersecurity by exploring previously limitedly explored strategies.

Discussion

Understanding how organizations successfully hire cybersecurity professionals remains important because of the current philosophy in the DoD of hiring contractors to do specialized work; however, DoD could grow an internal cybersecurity workforce instead of using a contracted workforce (Earle. Lippitz, Shapiro, & Van Atta, 2015). Overall costs are less when DoD contracts specialized work (Hefetz & Warner, 2004), but each time a contract changes, the potential to lose institutional knowledge exists (Bloodgood & Salisbury, 2001). In 2014, $445 billion of the US government budget went to contracting companies. The DoD received 64% of the $445 and service contracts accounted for 45% of DoD contract expenditures (Schwartz, Ginsberg, & Sargent, 2015). The DoD can make developing a cybersecurity workforce a reality by fixing the salary structure for cybersecurity professionals, developing new guidelines for recruiting for cybersecurity professionals, and injecting themselves into the training pipeline.

The first priority in the shift to growing a cybersecurity workforce for the DoD is to recognize and fix the salary structure. The best and brightest cyber warriors do not work for the U.S. government (Turk, 2013), because the U.S. government does not have the financial incentives to recruit and maintain top cybersecurity professionals (Choo, 2011). Cybersecurity professionals living in the Washington DC, Maryland, Virginia (DMV) corridor, for example, have the opportunity to earn six figure salaries (Morgan, 2016). The current government pay structure for DoD organizations in the DMV reaches six figures at the pay grade of GS 13 step 3, which is $101,116 per year (Government Pay Scale, n.d.). The U.S. government does offer a sense of stability in the workforce; however, the current political climate makes the level of stability impossible to guess over the next 5 to 10 years. DoD is also in constant competition with other government agencies, contracting companies and private sector information technology (IT) firms for the limited number of trained cybersecurity professionals (Turk, 2013). Finding a way to pay competitive salaries for cybersecurity professionals is an issue DoD needs to address to transition the DoD cybersecurity workforce.

The second priority is to change the way the government recruits the cybersecurity workforce. At security conferences like Blackhat, DefCON, ShmooCON, or any of the cybersecurity conferences across the United States, most of the presenters and the participants do not fit into the U.S. *government employee* mold (Long, 2012). Some of them are social outcasts (Long, 2012). However, the common thread among these cyber professionals is many are self-taught, many have above average technical aptitude, and many have a passion for the craft (Bratus, 2007). Cyber professionals spend hundreds of hours learning new tools, building new tools, learning new tactics, and finding ways to attack computers and networks successfully (Long, 2012). The training aptitude and motivation are present, however, the future cybersecurity professionals do not have the opportunity to obtain a position in the government because of the government focus on certification and education (Turk, 2013). Lowering or eliminating the barriers of entry into the government workforce may help the DoD recruit the cybersecurity professionals needed to transition the cybersecurity workforce

The last thing the DoD needs to add is more influence in the training pipeline for cybersecurity professionals (Turk, 2013). In 2016, job postings for cybersecurity positions required a bachelor's degree and certifications (Pierce, 2016). Future cybersecurity professionals may not have nor be interested in getting a bachelor's degree. Consequently, the DoD will need to find methods to train their cybersecurity workforce that do not include a 4-year degree. There is also a lack of standardization among the various cybersecurity programs offered (Paulsen, Mcduffie, Newhouse, & Toth, 2012). The cybersecurity programs available will give potential cybersecurity professionals a basic understand of serval cybersecurity topics, but the cybersecurity workforce will not have the specified training required by government and private companies to contribute to the organization on the first day of employment (Paulsen et al., 2012). The DoD's involvement in the training pipeline may allow the DoD to input the requirements DoD desires in a cybersecurity professional; which in turn, may help the DoD recruit and hire cybersecurity professionals pre equipped with the skillset to operate in DoD's cybersecurity workforce.

The DoD has the potential to lead the development and implementation of new, innovate techniques to train cybersecurity professionals. One method the DoD can explore for training is the use of cybersecurity competitions. Cybersecurity competitions allow students in training to put cybersecurity theories into action (Bei, Kesterson, Gwinnup, & Taylor, 2011). Preparing for competitions involves learning offensive and defensive cybersecurity tactics and techniques (Bei et al., 2011). A student in a college degree granting program can expect to have 1.5 years of training that focuses on the technical aspects of cybersecurity (McGettrick, 2013). Competing in competitions may provide the hands on experience in technical implementation and provide experience in researching vulnerabilities and techniques to exploit or defend against vulnerabilities in information systems.

Certification training is also an option (Turk, 2013). The threat of too many certifications on the market is a factor the DoD must consider when using this training method. Too many certifications offered by too many companies creates a situation that convolutes the understanding which certifications provide the best outcomes (Caldwell, 2013). Bachelor's degrees have a similar effect (Caldwell, 2013). Depending on the school they go to, the student may get some simulated experience, but the industry needs cybersecurity professionals that contribute to a security team the minute they are hired. For most programs, the students are only required to pass the courses taken. Having a bachelor's degree proves that the student completed a degree and has a general level of competence in the subject matter (Adams & Demaiter, 2008). Having certifications shows a level of ambition. The person has to study and understand the concepts to pass (Turk, 2013). They may not get everything they need from the certification process, but they have a starting point.

Programs exist for other U.S. government agencies and private organizations that the DoD should consider implementing on a larger scale. A good way to do this is to develop a cyber apprenticeship program. Apprenticeships have declined in the United States (Chen, 2014), but the training method has remained strong in European countries such as the United Kingdom (Caldwell, 2013). Apprenticeships are an effective method of training cybersecurity professionals (Caldwell, 2013). Higher education has a place, but that type of education would fit better for policy and management, not for the technical side of cyber operations (Turk, 2013). Adobe confronted their gap in training by developing an internal training program that increased the software developer's proficiency and increased the overall security culture of the organization (Kebbel-Wyen, 2012). The internal program consisted of four levels. Level one and level two were computer-based training and levels three and four were technical projects of varying lengths. Completion of the program is required before the developer moves to a software development team. After 2 years of implementing the program,

Adobe decreased the time of vulnerability mitigation from an average of 57 days to an average of 10 days (Kebbel-Wyen, 2012). The DoD can review programs such as the program at Adobe, as an example of a program that can help train cybersecurity professionals. The development of an apprenticeship program and internal training program may help the DoD transition to a majority government cybersecurity workforce.

Conclusion

Cybersecurity is an important function for every organization in the digital age. The level of importance increases for organizations such as the DoD where the safety of the United States may hang in the balance. A shortage of cybersecurity professionals exists across all industries, which forces hiring managers to compete with other contracting companies, other government agencies and private IT firms (Turk, 2013). Hiring managers may increase the ability to recruit and hire qualified cybersecurity professionals for DoD contracts if the hiring managers understand the contractual requirements and have a strong recruiting process (Pierce, 2016). Competition for cybersecurity professionals requires the DoD to rethink the current workforce model. Innovation will be a key factor in the DoD's strategy to institutionalize a self-sustaining cybersecurity workforce. Three things the DoD could do to build their own cybersecurity workforce are to (a) fix the pay structure, (b) fix the recruiting practices, and (c) get involved in the training pipeline. Increasing the number of U.S. government cybersecurity employees could create an environment that enhances the DoD's ability to protect the IT infrastructure sensitive data and information systems which is a recommendation that merits serious consideration moving forward.

THOUGHTS FROM THE ACADEMIC ENTREPRENEUR

The problem:

- Successfully hiring cybersecurity professionals for DoD contracts.

The goals:

- Understand the major considerations when hiring cybersecurity professionals.
- Offer alternatives to hiring contractors for DoD cybersecurity.

The questions to ask:

- What are the best methods for hiring cybersecurity professionals for DoD contracts?
- How can DoD change the current culture of using contractors to growing a cybersecurity workforce?

Today's Business Application:

- Hiring managers working on DoD cybersecurity contracts should understand all the requirements in the contract and hire candidates that met those requirements.
- Human resources plays a big role in the process and communication should be bi-directional to help avoid potential problems.
- DoD should review the current strategy for cybersecurity and consider changing how they operate to meet the demands of the future.

REFERENCES

Adams, T. L., & Demaiter, E. I. (2008). Skill, education and credentials in the new economy: the case of information technology workers. *Work, Employment, & Society, 22,* 351–362. doi:10.1177/0950017008089109

Argyris, C. (1976). Theories of action that inhibit individual learning. *American Psychologist, 31,* 638–654. doi:10.1037/0003-066X.31.9.638

Argyris, C. (1996). Crossroads: Unrecognized defenses of scholars: Impact on theory and research. *Organization Science, 7,* 79–87. doi:10.1287/orsc.7.1.79

Bloodgood, J. M., & Salisbury, W. D. (2001). Understanding the influence of organizational change strategies on information technology and knowledge management strategies. *Decision Support Systems, 31*(1), 55–69. doi:10.1016/S0167-9236(00)00119-6

Bureau of Labor and Statistics. (BLS). (2016). *Information security analyst.* Retrieved from https://www.bls.gov/

Bratus, S. (2007). Hacker curriculum: How hackers learn networking. *IEEE Distributed Systems Online, 8*(10), 1–7. doi:10.1109/MDSO.2007.4384582

Burley, D. L., Eisenberg, J., & Goodman, S. E. (2014). Would cybersecurity professionalization help address the cybersecurity crisis? *Communications of the ACM, 57*(2), 24–27. doi:10.1145/2556936

Caldwell, T. (2013). Plugging the cybersecurity skills gap. *Computer Fraud & Security.* Retrieved from http://digital-library.theiet.org/

Chen, R. (2014). The decline of localized education in the United States: A new age of bureaucratization. *Comparative Advantage, 2*(1), 36–46. Retrieved from https://economics.stanford.edu/

Choo, K. K. R. (2011). The cyber threat landscape: Challenges and future research directions. *Computers & Security, 30,* 719–731. doi:10.1016/j.cose.2011.08.004

Cobert, B. (2016). *Strengthening the federal cybersecurity workforce: The OPM director's blog.* Retrieved from https://www.opm.gov

Day, B. (2014, September 4). *Cybersecurity commission education and workforce workgroup first meeting minutes.* Retrieved from https://cyberva.virginia.gov/

Drtil, J. (2013). Impact of information security incidents: Theory and reality. *Journal of Systems Integration, 4*(1), 44–52. Retrieved from http://si-journal.org

Dunn Cavelty, M. (2014). Breaking the cybersecurity dilemma: Aligning security needs and removing vulnerabilities. *Science and Engineering Ethics, 20,* 701–715. doi:10.1007/s11948-014-9551

Earle, C.R., Kelly, J. C., Leader, P., Earle, C. R., Lippitz, M. J., Shapiro, B. A., & Atta, R. H. Van. (2015). *Contracting for knowledge-based and equipment-related services*. Retrieved from http://www.acq.osd.mil

Hefetz, A., & Warner, M. (2004). Privatization and its reverse: Explaining the dynamics of the government contracting process. *Journal of Public Administration Research and Theory, 14*(2), 171–190. doi:10.1093/jopart/muh012

Ifinedo, P. (2014). Information systems security policy compliance: An empirical study of the effects of socialization, influence, and cognition. *Information & Management, 51*(1), 69–79. https://dx.doi.org/10.1016/j.im.2013.10.001

International Information Systems Security Certification Consortium (ISC)2. (2016.). *CISSP-Certified Information Systems Security Professional*. Retrieved from http://www.isc2.org

Johnson, G., Wilding, P., & Robson, A. (2014). Can outsourcing recruitment deliver satisfaction?: A hiring manager perspective. *Personnel Review, 43*, 303–326. doi:10.1108/PR-12-2012-0212

Long, L. (2012). *Profiling hackers*. Retrieved from https://www.sans.org

Kumar, R., & Singh, H. (2012). Analysis of information systems security issues and security techniques. *International Journal of Advanced Computer Research, 2*(6), 65–68. Retrieved from http://theaccents.org/

Morgan, S. (2016, January 09). *Top cybersecurity salaries in U.S. metros hit $380,000*. Retrieved from http://www.forbes.com

Nielsen, S. C. (2012). Pursuing security in cyberspace: Strategic and organizational challenges. *Orbis, 56*, 336–356. doi:10.1016/j.orbis.2012.05.004

Pay & Leave Salaries & Wages. (n.d.). Retrieved from https://www.opm.gov

Pierce, A. O. (2016). Exploring the cybersecurity hiring gap (Doctoral dissertation). Available from Dissertations & Theses @ Walden University. (UMI No. 1848667353)

Strohmeier, S. (2013). Employee relationship management: Realizing competitive advantage through information technology. *Human Resource Management Review, 23*, 93–104. doi:10.1016/j.hrmr.2012.06.009

Suby, M., & Dickson, F. (2015). *The 2015 (ISC)² global information security workforce study*. Retrieved from http://www.isc2cares.org

Turk, R. (2013). *Preparing a cybersecurity workforce for the 21st century. U.S. Army War College*. Retrieved from http://oai.dtic.mil/

Von Solms, R., & Van Niekerk, J. (2013). From information security to cybersecurity professionals. *Computers & Security, 3*, 97–102. doi:10.1016/j.cose.2013.04.004

Yixin, L. (2011). Study on the current situation of information security and countermeasures in China. *Energy Procedia, 5*, 392–396. doi:10.1016/j.egypro.2011.03.067

About the Author...

Dr. Adam O. Pierce hails from Smithfield, VA and currently lives in Chesapeake, VA. Dr. Adam holds several information security certifications including; Certified Information Systems Security Professional (CISSP), Certified Information Systems Auditor (CISA), Certified Penetration Tester (CPT), Security +, Network + and Linux +. His higher educational degrees are; a Bachelor of Arts (BA) in History from Old Dominion University; a Master of Science (MS) in Network and Communications Management from the Keller Graduate School of Management; a Master of Business Administration (MBA) from Walden University; and a Doctorate of Business Administration (DBA) from Walden University.

Dr. Adam is an Adjunct Associate Professor at the University of Maryland University College (UMUC), where he has taught Network Security, *Fundamentals of Networking, Ethical Hacking,* and *Linux Administration.* Nothing brings him more joy than seeing his students learn. He is a member of the Urban League of Hampton Roads Young Professionals, ISACA, and ISC2.

Dr. Adam is an Information Systems Security Analyst at NASA's Langley Research Center in Hampton, VA. He is also the CEO and Founder of Pierce & Long LLC., an information technology and cybersecurity startup company. His doctoral study, *Exploring the Cybersecurity Hiring Gap,* provided a glimpse into the processes used by successful hiring managers in companies that provide cybersecurity services to DoD and provided him with a unique opportunity to gain valuable insight into DoD contracting.

To reach Dr. Adam O. Pierce for information on consulting or doctoral coaching, please e-mail: piercea45@gmail.com

CHAPTER 4

Using Cryptocurrencies to Fund Small Business: Managing the Cybersecurity Risks

Dr. Ivan Salaberrios

Small businesses are increasingly challenged to find money to fund their operations (Salaberrios, 2016). Depending on the state of the economy, a small business owner may or may not have a comfortable experience locating a suitable source of funding. Most small business owners usually have a more difficult path forward aligning with a financial partner. These complexities seem to be nonexistent when considering cryptocurrency as a source of funding. When comparing the use of traditional currency to cryptocurrency, small businesses experience a greater upside to funding their business with cryptocurrency because of the lower costs and decentralization associated with cryptocurrencies such as Bitcoin and E-cash (Extance, 2015). The process and rules that come with borrowing traditional currency are widely known. Most people witness others experience the challenges to borrowing money throughout the course of their lives. Cryptocurrency is relatively new and used extensively with Internet businesses. One should be opportunistic with refractive thinking to improve funding options by addressing cybersecurity vulnerabilities. Entrepreneurs need to have better understanding about the processing rules for obtaining cryptocurrency when compared to borrowing traditional monies. However, cryptocurrency is less challenging to get, and the costs are significantly less (Ametrano, 2016). Approaching this chapter with refractive thinking, one can explore the removal of boundaries such as cost of money, credit-based eligibility, and accessibility to capital. One can study a business problem where a small business can access funding without a bank or a dollar. Refractive thinking encourages research through a lens without limits. Cryptocurrency provides a similar access. However, cryptocurrency has significant cybersecurity risks and documented vulnerabilities. In this chapter, the research explores beyond the use of cryptocurrencies into when regulation does exist. Using refractive thinking to examine the use of cryptocurrencies by entrepreneurs to fund their business. Entrepreneurs can replace traditional funding programs using cryptocurrencies such as Bitcoin. Cryptocurrencies may substitute special funding programs such as invoice factoring as well. The goal of this chapter is to examine the cybersecurity risks small businesses must address when considering using cryptocurrency.

Although many advantages to cryptocurrency exist, significant disadvantages remain that are unique to cryptocurrency when compared to traditional funding. The principal problems with cryptocurrency are the cybersecurity risks. Bergman (2015) conducted a survey showing that 82% of U.S. citizens worried about data breaches with banks. A separate survey showed 77% of consumers thought notification of exposure was important (Bergman, 2015). Cryptocurrencies like Bitcoin have been in existence for 9 years increasing in price from $0 to more than $650 (Luther, 2016). By reviewing the cryptocurrencies that are available, one can examine the current management gaps associated with cryptocurrency. The purpose of this chapter is to determine if the risks to small businesses are manageable by implementing cybersecurity planning to address the cryptocurrency risks.

Cybersecurity

Cybersecurity is an entire science of its own. The knowledge limits of the cybersecurity are not well defined. Experts have exhaustive approaches which often overlap (Prasad & Arumugam, 2016). Specific standards of expert cybersecurity skill level does not exist (Singer & Friedman, 2014). With that in mind, cybersecurity experts do not agree on a standard of implementation. Therefore, users are on their own to decide their level and value of their respective protections (Dunn Cavelty, 2014). Cyber insurance is in the beginning phases of deployment across mainstream businesses. More clients require their suppliers to carry cybersecurity insurance. Most cybersecurity insurance rates depend on the value of protected data.

Various definitions across the world exists to describe cybersecurity. More broadly, cybersecurity is the technology used to protect other forms of technology (Prasad & Arumugam, 2016). The proper formation of cybersecurity protection requires planning. Small businesses should include cybersecurity somewhere business or strategic planning (Clozel, 2016). The appropriate level of cybersecurity should correlate with the degree of exposure users have to the Internet. The focus of this chapter is small businesses overcoming the inherent risks of storing digital currency on their network whether on-premise or using a third-party cloud (Varriale, 2013). By managing the inherent risk with a comprehensive cybersecurity strategy, entrepreneurs can feasibly use cryptocurrency to fund their business activities (Salaberrios, 2016).

Cryptocurrency

Cryptocurrency has not caught on to mainstream markets, especially small businesses. Similar to cybersecurity, education about cryptocurrency and its use is unknown. Few experts can consult on the use of cryptocurrency effectively (Brown, 2016). Few cryptocurrency experts exist that understand how to utilize digital currency for small business activities. The concept of electronic cash emerged three decades ago; however, the confidence of entrepreneurs to use cryptocurrency still has not reached an acceptable level (White, 2015). Researchers believe a lack of security and knowledge about the future of cryptocurrency correlates to consumer confidence. Cyber criminals use cryptocurrency because of their anonymous attributes (Extance, 2015). However, studies have shown the risk of anonymity by users are manageable and do not pose a significant cybersecurity vulnerability.

E-cash

E-cash is a concept founded in 1983. David Chaum published a paper in 1983 detailing the idea of the anonymous electronic money system (Lewis, 1996). The details included the E-cash software being stored on a user's local computer as cash but in a digital format. Banks used cryptology to sign the E-cash. The E-cash system is a cryptographic electronic money system intended to operate anonymously (Lian, Chen, & Li, 2014).

According to Extance (2015), David Chaum founded Digicash in 1990. E-cash is a predecessor to cryptocurrencies. Digicash is the earliest of digital currencies. Bitcoin has managed to build on the founding concept of E-cash. The purpose of E-cash was to give consumers privacy and more safety (Lian, Chen, & Li, 2014). The digital currency was successful in providing anonymity, but fell short of its security goals. E-cash managed to create an emergence of vulnerabilities that are still being addressed today (Phillips, 1998). From the inception of the E-cash concept, existed vulnerabilities with the whole electronic money idea (Yacobi, 2001). Some solutions have emerged to counter the security weaknesses of E-cash. Experts in cryptology have proposed restrictive blind signatures that consist of a partially blind signature scheme with conditional properties. Such solutions introduce discrete logarithm in sequence-based schemes to secure the random nature of public key signatures that introduced key vulnerabilities (Qiu, Gong, Liu, Long, & Chen, 2011). Current cryptographic solutions build on past proposals and attempt to solve the exploited weaknesses to E-cash. Partial real-time audits by Yacobi (2001), is one example of many solutions developed from ideas based on risk management policies.

Bitcoin

David Chaum's company, Digicash, closed its doors in 1998. Experts believe that digital cash was not able to overcome industry objectives to the security vulnerabilities. As a result of the cybersecurity vulnerabilities, financial sector developed regulations to address the cybersecurity breaches with E-cash (Backhouse, 1998). The regulations are an indirect result of the closing of its doors. According to Turpin (2013), the E-cash concept hit the market way too early. The solutions available in the 1990s were not robust enough to sustain consumer confidence. Digicash relied on a Trusted Third Party (TPP) base system, which eventually becomes a lost cause. Through the technical advances in cryptology and evolution of the Internet, the idea of Bitcoin was able to emerge (Angel & McCabe, 2015).

Satoshi Nakamoto introduced the first idea of the Bitcoin in 2008 (Prentis, 2015). Mr. Nakamoto is an anonymous person who posted a white paper online that detail the framework of the Bitcoin. The Bitcoin design introduced the framework for cryptocurrency (Negurita, 2014). Research is not clear as to why the founder of Bitcoin chose to publish anonymously. The founder's real identity is still unknown. All of the Bitcoin in circulation in 2016 is worth over $7 billion (Extance, 2015).

According to Extance (2015), Bitcoin is the first cryptocurrency created. At its core, Bitcoin is a peer-to-peer electronic cash system. The peer-to-peer concept mirrors the file share network that uses media such as music and videos. Its purpose was to prevent double spending. This cryptocurrency has no central authority, defined as decentralized, having no middle entity or clearinghouse such as a traditional currency. Unlike digital cash, Bitcoin does not rely on a trusted third-party-based system (Angel & McCabe, 2015). In comparison, the Bitcoin as a cryptocurrency relies on a non-trust-based system which gives the Bitcoin its decentralized characteristics. The innovation of the decentralization solution was a significant achievement of which cryptocurrency emerged.

The basic concept of cryptocurrency is unknown by many experts in the financial industry (Iwamura, Kitamura, & Matsumoto, 2014). Satoshi Nakamoto's primary innovation was to obtain a digital agreement by inventing the ability to rewrite the ledger, not allowing the spending of the same transaction twice (Extance, 2016). The innovation did not require a central authority. By not having a central authority the Bitcoin innovation created competition for transactions.

Users refer to the transaction competition as mining (Prentis, 2015). The process of mining for Bitcoin creates a virtual marketplace. The number of miners in the world estimates to be over 100,000 nodes. The number of miners correlates with the current Bitcoin prices. The Bitcoin network is secure because of the number of miners operating in the peer to peer network. The miners are responsible for approving the transactions to ensure fairness, stability, and network security (Turpin, 2013). Bitcoin regulation does not exist; therefore, the number of miners is not official.

Mining and the Blockchain

In a peer-to-peer network, all of the participants in the network possess a history of all transactions. The participants in a Bitcoin peer-to-peer network refer to themselves as miners (Hughes & Middlebrook, 2015). At the core of the transaction is the account balances. By using public key cryptography, the transaction files simply state receipt of the transaction and from where the transaction came. Once a signed transaction has a public key encryption, the transaction transmits to all of the participants in the network from one peer. All transactions require confirmation by miners (Turpin, 2013). Cryptocurrency concept builds on the confirmation process. Unconfirmed transactions remain in a pending status. Once confirmed, a transaction becomes part of a list of past transactions known as a blockchain. The participants in the peer-to-peer network, also called miners, are the only ones who can confirm a transaction (Varriale, 2013). After a miner confirms a transaction, other nodes in the network add to the database which becomes a part of the blockchain. Miners receive a commission payment in Bitcoins. Miners use and SHA 256–algorithm as the basis of a cryptology puzzle. Solving the puzzle of an unconfirmed transaction allows the miner to add to the blockchain to create a Bitcoin (Yli-Huumo, Ko, Choi, Park, & Smolander, 2016).

Seemingly, Bitcoins create value out of thin air. The average rate of Bitcoin creation is six per hour. The number of Bitcoin does not exceed 22 million (Turpin, 2013). The amount of Bitcoin is finite. However, the money supply associated with Bitcoin can exceed a value of 22 million dollars because of fractional-reserve banking. As a result, cryptocurrencies are susceptible to the same effects as traditional money such as inflation and deflation (Prentis, 2015). Cryptocurrencies keep a database across a peer-to-peer network. No involvement of a central server or database is not required. Peers confirm all transactions in the network. The transactional properties have its security such as each transaction be irreversible and pseudonymous. Permits or regulations are not required to use cryptocurrency. Bitcoin uses an open source software that is available at no cost. Cryptocurrencies are unique when compared to traditional currency because they do not require any securities other than the complicated math confirm a transaction and add to the block chain (White, 2015). By definition, the Bitcoin establishes itself as a real currency used to spend on physical items in the real world (Varriale, 2013). One of the keys to success will be making cryptocurrency less complicated for large-scale integration into global markets (Granger, 2014).

Risks and Vulnerabilities

Cryptocurrency is digital money created from code. For example, Bitcoin is a string of encryption that encodes to represent a single unit of currency. Like any software, cryptocurrency has encryption vulnerabilities. Many of the associated vulnerabilities with cryptocurrency are manageable (Dunn Cavelty, 2014). Other vulnerabilities with Bitcoin and cyber currency are driven by the market changes and therefore unmanageable. For example, the volatility in the value of a Bitcoin. The rate of exchange has been a concern to people who exchange currency and has caused down in its validity as a currency. The decentralization of cryptocurrency brings regulatory concerns to mainstream users as well as small businesses (Check Hayden, 2015). The lack of regulation is a major risk to companies that are considering to use cryptocurrency. Without regulation, businesses do not have any consumer rights or customer protection under the law, therefore, leaving itself exposed to cybersecurity risks. Traditional financial institutions refused to recognize cryptocurrencies until regulation exists by way of centralization (Prentis, 2015).

Cybersecurity Risks of Using Cryptocurrencies

Bitcoin and cryptocurrency of vulnerable to cyber-crimes all over the world (Brown, 2016). Users can not alter cryptocurrency at the unit level. Users can steal cryptocurrency or obtain Bitcoin fraudulently like a traditional currency. Cryptocurrency must reside on a user node, and storage of cryptocurrency will be like keeping cash on the premises of a brick-and-mortar business. Physically business owners do not keep significant amounts of cash on his person. Business owners do not alert the outside world to the presence of money in a building or office. Such information would provoke criminals to commit crimes trying to steal the cash (Hughes & Middlebrook, 2015). A similar concern exists with cybersecurity. Hackers may not be able to alter the currency, but they are equally motivated to attack users who knowingly keep significant amounts of cryptocurrency. The motivation of hackers to cyber-attacks on businesses. Physically business owners and consumers can store or record their currency values in a traditional bank. Banking institutions are accountable for the security of the currency. Banks have made significant strides to secure money and protect digital assets such as electronic credits transactional history (Bitam, Zeadally, & Mellouk, 2016). Cryptocurrency poses the same risks to currency holders as traditional currency.

According to Brown (2016), the attraction to cryptocurrency by criminal actors is the anonymity. The digital currency rarely traces back to an actual individual. Cyber criminals prefer the use of digital currencies because they can elude criminal justice professionals such as law enforcement. Bitcoin has been lauded as low risk and incapable of money laundering schemes. Herein lies the conflict between currency experts. A study by Check Hayden (2015) supported the use of a solid cybersecurity plan. Check Hayden (2015) does not agree with Brown (2016), stating that users can fight cybercrime effectively. However, no centralized security exists for cryptocurrency other than existing tools for cybersecurity. Small businesses can plan against cyber-attacks to protect their cryptocurrency as would any traditional bank by implementing a cybersecurity plan. A good cybersecurity plan can help protect small businesses against the increased risk of attacks when using cryptocurrency (Carr, 2016).

Small Business and Cryptocurrency

Small businesses have yet to catch on to the advantages of using cryptocurrency to fund their business. Partially the hesitation of entrepreneurs comes from the volatility in the value of cryptocurrency. The risk of managing cryptocurrency is a topic of great concern for entrepreneurs (Varriale, 2013). However, as recognition of Bitcoin grows, cryptocurrencies will become an obvious choice for small businesses to find their operations. More research and studies will be available for small businesses to access and learn about managing the risks associated with storing and protecting against cybersecurity risks. Both public and private firms have similar incentive to build cybersecurity strategies (Clozel, 2016). Small businesses incorporate cybersecurity planning to address vulnerabilities and anticipate cyber-attacks to protect their cryptocurrencies (Carr, 2016). In the future, finance experts will propose a regulation for cryptocurrency. The direct conflict between implementing regulation and deploying cybersecurity is the centralization.

Regulating Cryptocurrency for Small Business Use

Decentralization is the core concept of cryptocurrency. The absence of a centralization is why cryptocurrencies like Bitcoin exist in the currency markets today. According to Varriale (2013), the greatest fear of regulation is the loss of anonymity. Users and transactions being anonymous are at the heart of risks concerns with cryptocurrency. Regulation of cryptocurrency may have to focus on the financial gateways or any point where businesses or users need to convert to traditional currency. No regulation exists for cryptocurrencies. When officials propose and implement regulations, the regulations will have to focus on intersecting or overlapping features of crypto and traditional currencies (Varriale, 2013). Ideally, this means wherever the conversion of cryptocurrencies take place with online services like PayPal, Amazon, etc. Realizing the full cycle of obtaining currency one can see a small business's ability to acquire funds as well as transact debits and credits. Keep in mind that the study by Varriale doubts the future viability of cryptocurrency. The study goes on to question the level of popularity and calls for the control of cryptocurrency. By understanding the full cycle of a transaction, small business managers can use a critical and refractive thinking process to develop cybersecurity plans that will address any vulnerabilities in such cycles. Entrepreneurs should be opportunistic using critical and refractive thinking to close the wide gap of successful businesses that fail due to poor financial literacy (Salaberrios, 2016). Therefore, managing cryptocurrency security risks to acceptable levels (White, 2015). White (2015) disagrees with Varriale (2013) as well as Prentis (2015). The research conducted by White supported a digital market for cryptocurrencies supporting level of security as acceptable for business use. Such acceptability should create confidence in the marketplace for small business owners to use cryptocurrencies regularly as they would traditional money.

The ability for small businesses to have another option to fund their activities may positively change the entrepreneurial landscape soon. By not having to use traditional funding processes, entrepreneurs will be able to seek to fund in ways that replace special funding programs. Business owners can replace invoice factoring and asset-based lending with some of the cryptocurrencies available on the market. Cryptocurrencies such as Bitcoin cost less to obtain (Varriale, 2013). The number of businesses that use cryptocurrency grows with the recognition of cryptocurrencies in traditional business markets. In an academic study conducted by Salaberrios (2016), small businesses had a positive effect when using invoice factoring to fund their activities. The results of this study showed that small businesses do not require as much capital to fund their operations. Invoice factoring provides a small business the ability to sustain their operations. Cryptocurrencies may replace small business funding program such as factoring. Cryptocurrencies may become a primary source of financing as availability in the marketplace continues to grow (Varriale, 2013). The understanding that an entrepreneur requires managing finances will change as well. A business owner may not need to become a financial wizard for their business to be successful or at least not go under prematurely due to a lack of financial literacy (Salaberrios, 2016).

Areas of future study may include researching the limits of revenue before a small business may need to utilize traditional currency (Clozel, 2016). Does a threshold exist that shows traditional money having advantages over cryptocurrencies? If a threshold does exist, does limitations of cybersecurity determine the feasibility of maintaining cryptocurrency versus utilizing the security features of a traditional banking system? Will users have access to tools that will enable them to protect their cryptocurrency as well as any traditional currency clearinghouse? These questions provide a good direction to studying cybersecurity planning with regards to small businesses utilizing cryptocurrencies in the future.

Conclusion

The need for a cybersecurity plan for small businesses using cryptocurrency presents a significant opportunity for consulting services. Access to cryptocurrencies for small businesses is growing. More entrepreneurs can use solid advice from researchers about cryptocurrencies. Researchers can advise various methods to using cryptocurrencies to fund a small business. A growing number of cryptocurrencies exist that compete with Bitcoin in E-cash. Cybersecurity vulnerabilities will emerge with the growing number of different kinds of cryptocurrencies. Small businesses will be able to replace existing traditional banking options by choosing to fund their activities with some form of cryptocurrency. However, storing cryptocurrencies presents a cybersecurity challenge that most small businesses are not prepared to meet. This chapter gave a refractive thinking analysis of small businesses use of cryptocurrencies as a means of funding their operations.

THOUGHTS FROM THE ACADEMIC ENTREPRENEUR

The problem to be solved:
- Cybersecurity risks using cryptocurrency to fund small business.

The goals:
- Better understanding of cybersecurity risks associated with cryptocurrency.
- Effectively manage cybersecurity risks so small businesses can reap the benefits of cryptocurrencies.

The questions to ask:
- What are the major risks when using cryptocurrencies to fund small business?
- Can a small business create a security strategy to manage major risks inherent to cryptocurrency?

Today's Business Application:
- Understanding the major risks involved with cryptocurrencies are manageable and can be effectively minimized with a cybersecurity plan.
- Security planning is essential to managing the cybersecurity risks with cryptocurrency.
- Understanding that small businesses can benefit from using cryptocurrency and not experience any more risks when compared to using traditional currency.

REFERENCES

Ametrano, F. M. (2016). *Hayek money: The cryptocurrency price stability solution*. Retrieved from https://ssrn.com/abstract=2425270

Angel, J. J., & McCabe, D. (2015). The ethics of payments: Paper, plastic, or bitcoin? *Journal of Business Ethics, 132*, 603–611. http://dx.doi.org/10.1007/s10551-014-2354-x

Backhouse, J. P. (1998). Security: The achilles heel of electronic commerce. *Society, 35*(4), 28–31. Retrieved from: http://eprints.lse.ac.uk/27029/

Bergman, K. M. (2015). A target to the heart of the first amendment: Government endorsement of responsible disclosure as unconstitutional. *Journal of International Human Rights, 13*(2), 117–151. Retrieved from http://scholarlycommons.law.northwestern.edu/njihr/

Bitam, S., Zeadally, S., & Mellouk, A. (2016). Bio-inspired cybersecurity for wireless sensor networks. *IEEE Communications Magazine, 54*(6), 68–74. doi:10.1109/mcom.2016.7497769

Brown, S. D. (2016). Cryptocurrency and criminality. *The Police Journal, 89*, 327–339. doi:10.1177/0032258X16658927

Carr, M. (2016). Public-private partnerships in national cybersecurity strategies. *International Affairs, 92*(1), 43–62. doi:10.1111/1468-2346.12504

Check, E. (2015). Cybercrime fighters target human error. *Nature, 518*(7539), 282–283. doi:10.1038/518282a

Clozel, L. (2016). How treasury is trying to shape state digital currency regs. *American Banker, 181*(61), 1. Retrieved from http://www.castconsultants.com/wp-content/uploads/2016/04

Dunn Cavelty, M. (2014). Breaking the cybersecurity dilemma: Aligning security needs and removing vulnerabilities. *Science & Engineering Ethics, 20*, 701–715. doi:10.1007/s11948-014-9551-y

Extance, A. (2015). The future of cryptocurrencies: Bitcoin and beyond. *Nature, 526*(7571), 21–23. doi:10.1038/526021a

Granger, S. (2014). *The digital mystique: How the culture of connectivity can empower your life-online and off*. Seal Press.

Hughes, S. J., & Middlebrook, S. T. (2015). Advancing a framework for regulating cryptocurrency payments intermediaries. *Yale Journal on Regulation, 32*, 495–559. Retrieved from http://yalejreg.com

Iwamura, M., Kitamura, Y., & Matsumoto, T. (2014). *Is bitcoin the only cryptocurrency in the town? Economics of Cryptocurrency and Friedrich A. Hayek*. http://dx.doi.org/10.2139/ssrn.2405790

Lewis J., W. (1996). The power of the pachyderm: Currency traders and the new gold standard. *Journal of Financial Planning, 9*(6), 38. Retrieved from https://www.onefpa.org/journal

Lian, B., Chen, G., & Li, J. (2014). Provably secure E-cash system with practical and efficient complete tracing. *International Journal of Information Security, 13*(3), 271–289. doi:10.1007/s10207-014-0240-2

Luther, W. J. (2016). Bitcoin and the future of digital payments. *Independent Review, 20,* 397–404. Retrieved from http://www.independent.org/publications/tir/

Negurita, O. (2014). Bitcoin: Between legal and financial performance. *Contemporary Readings in Law and Social Justice, 6*(1), 242–248. Retrieved from http://ezproxy.occlib.nocccd.edu/login?url=http://link.galegroup.com/apps/doc/A379981842/OVIC?u=occc_main&xid=3ce8c81b

Phillips, D. J. (1998). The social construction of a secure, anonymous electronic payment system: frame alignment and mobilization around Ecash. *Journal of Information Technology, 13*(4), 273–284. http://dx.doi.org/10.1057/jit.1998.6

Prasad, A. R., & Arumugam, S. (2016). *Cybersecurity: Beyond 2050 Wireless World in 2050 and Beyond: A Window into the Future!* (pp. 129–136): Switzerland: Springer.

Prentis, M. (2015). Digital metal: Regulating bitcoin as a commodity. *Case Western Reserve Law Review, 66,* 609–638. Retrieved from http://scholarlycommons.law.case.edu/cgi/viewcontent.cgi?article=2654&context=caselrev

Qiu, W., Gong, Z., Liu, B., Long, Y., & Chen, K. (2011). Restrictive partially blind signature for resource-constrained information systems. *Knowledge and Information Systems, 26*(1), 87–103. http://dx.doi.org/10.1007/s10115-009-0273-4

Salaberrios, I. J. (2016). *The effects of using invoice factoring to fund a small business.* Retrieved from http://pqdtopen.proquest.com/doc/1761840902.html?FMT=ABS

Singer, P. W., & Friedman, A. (2014). *Cybersecurity: What everyone needs to know.* New York, NY: Oxford University Press.

Turpin, J. B. (2013). Bitcoin: The economic case for a global, virtual currency operating in an unexplored legal framework. *Indiana Journal of Global Legal Studies, 21,* 335–368. Retrieved from http://www.repository.law.indiana.edu/ijgls/vol21/iss1/13

Varriale, G. (2013). Bitcoin: How to regulate a virtual currency. *International Financial Law Review, 43*(1), 3–7. Retrieved from http://www.iflr.com/Article/3245397/Banking/

White, L. H. (2015). The market for cryptocurrencies. *CATO Journal, 35*, 383–402. Retrieved from https://object.cato.org/sites/cato.org/files/serials/files/cato-journal/2015/5/cj-v35n2-13.pdf

Yacobi, Y. (2001). Risk management for e-cash systems with partial real-time audit. *Netnomics : Economic Research and Electronic Networking, 3*(2), 119. doi:10.1023/A:1011403312992

Yli-Huumo, J., Ko, D., Choi, S., Park, S., & Smolander, K. (2016). Where is current research on blockchain technology? A systematic review. *PLoS One, 11*(10). doi:10.1371/journal.pone.0163477

About the Author...

Dr. Ivan Salaberrios resides in Pickerington, Ohio. Dr. Ivan holds several accredited degrees; a Bachelor of Technical Management (BTM) from DeVry University; a Master of Business Administration (MBA) from Keller Graduate School; and a Doctorate of Business Administration (DBA) from Walden University. Dr. Ivan also is a certified Project Management Professional (PMP) and Lean Six Sigma Black Belt Certified.

Dr. Ivan is the CEO and founder of AIM Technical Consultants. His career in the telecommunications industry began as a field engineer working with AMPs Radio Equipment, where he obtained extensive experience in RF Engineering, Network Engineering and Project Management.

In 17 years, Dr. Ivan has grown AIM from a handful of engineers to one of the largest staffing and engineering firms focused exclusively in wireless telecom. This growth is largely attributable to Ivan's relationship-building skills, dedication to exceptional service delivery, and unwavering focus on continuous improvement. Dr. Ivan is a Gulf War veteran, serving an enlistment term in the U.S. Navy on the USS Yorktown CG-48. He was honorably discharged in 1992.

To reach Dr. Ivan Salaberrios for information on consulting or doctoral coaching, please e-mail: ivans@aimtechinc.com

About the Company...

AIM Technical Consultants has experienced significant wireless industry growth since opening for business in 1999. We attribute this proven track record to our ability to consistently deliver IT field management and wireless technology implementation, allowing our customers peace of mind. Add to that our dedication to providing the best technical and professional services in the industry and AIM Technical Consultant's commitment to positioning ourselves as the *go to* wireless industry service provider, and the results speak for themselves. AIM Technical provides services in IT and wireless telecommunications committed to delivering unparalleled Cloud Engineering life-cycle support to our demanding customers with specific IT and wireless telecommunication needs.

    For more information, please contact email: office@aimtechnical.com phone: 614-452-773 website: https://www.aimtechnical.com

CHAPTER 5

Challenges of Setting Policy to Reduce Cyber Attacks in the Information Technology Industry

Dr. Loyce Chithambo

According to Chithambo (2011), the use of web services continues to increase with the increase of information security breaches in many industries, including the industries in this study: finance, health-care, automotive, technology, and the airlines. Online service increased as companies strive to reduce costs, increase profits, and remain locally and globally competitive, though this has also led to increased incidences of data breaches and identity theft. Privacy and security incidents pose a serious risk for a company's business accomplishments, causing economic impacts to companies and individuals. Most research confirms that with the increase in web services, information security breaches continue to increase (Nofer, Hinz, Muntermann, & Rossnagel, 2014).

Portable devices are major targets for hackers, which is concerning because as the need and use of wireless portable devices continues to increase, resulting in an increase of mobile malware and viruses, increased complexity in malware (Suarez, Guillermo, Tapiador, & Lombardi Di Piertro, 2014). Because breaches continue to increase on wireless devices, privacy is at high risk (Nofer, 2014), including the health care industry, resulting in many breaches that go undetected.

Information security is a growing concern in the healthcare industry, as described by Blanke and McGrady (2016). The Federal Emergency Management Agency (FEMA) identified cyber-attacks as an emerging concern. Because of the concern, some regulations like the Health Insurance Portability and Accountability Act (HIPAA) and the Health Information Technology for Economic and Clinical Health Act (HITECH) have increased security requirements and are enforcing compliance through stiff financial penalties.

According to Chithambo (2011), technology changes are rapid, as portable devices are changing with the technological needs. An example of the rapid technological changes is that, in less than a decade portable devices included PDAs, and cell phones; smartphones and tablets are among the common mobile devices, Musheer and Sheeraz (2014) described a smartphone as a combination of a PDA and telephone with a more powerful CPU, with more RAM, more storage space, and speed. An iPhone is a most popular smart phone credited for changing the industry forever. The risk is that once lost, these devices contain a wealth of information that could be compromised. Any mobile device is subject to loss. A smart phone carries more information, which means if a mobile is lost the risk is many more times than the risk of simply losing contacts and text messages. Malware is cited as among the most common software attacking mobile phones exposed to hacking risks stresses (Liao & Zen, 2014).

Many industries including finance, health-care, automotive, technology, and the airlines use portable mobile devices for quick information access, instant communication, and improved organization. Other institutions such as those in higher education (post-secondary education) also use smart phones for educational purposes. The emphasis on information privacy remains the same because information residing online is vulnerable. As discussed by Chithambo (2011) in earlier incidences of hacked firms such as OfficeMax and Barnes & Noble, hackers tapped into unprotected networks, allowing hackers from different countries to acquire credit card information through unsecured wireless network communications. Additionally, some retail stores were victims of cyber-attack costing companies money, putting individual identities at risk; these retail stores included Target, Sears, and Kmart (Kantor, 2013; Manworren, Letwat, & Daily, 2016).

Cyber-attacks are costly both to individuals and organizations. The Target breach took place during the 2013 holiday shopping season. The breach affected the credit card information of 40 million people. Chithambo (2011, 2015) stated that with these additional incidents of cybersecurity breaches, the need for organizations to cut costs and remain competitive in the global market increased as well. Chithambo continued to emphasize that the primary concern in unprotected networks is that hackers continue to target and intercept information transmitted through portable devices. Employees can easily transfer portable devices outside of their protected areas, subjecting the devices to theft. However, the fact remains that organizations need to enforce policies that tighten the security of the individual as well as the company.

The Chithambo (2011) qualitative study explored policies and procedures available to protect proprietary information when individuals use portable devices. The in-depth interviews included information technology leaders from each of the following industries: finance, health care, automotive, technology, and airline, for a total of 20 participants. The participating leaders were in charge of information security within their respective industries. The industries were located within a 100-mile radius in the Dallas Metroplex. The criteria for analysis included leaders' perceptions on how company information is protected from unauthorized use as individuals work from home.

Background of the Problem

According to Chithambo (2011, 2015), data security is vital in an electronically mediated work because of open network communication security breaches and identity theft have surged with the increase in the development of portable telecommuting devices. Bhagoliwal and Karjee (2016) confirmed that smart phones, tablets, and personal computers improve productivity and bring a competitive advantage for businesses, creating a need to enhance personal safety when individuals travel in remote locations. Telecommuters can work remotely with convenience, allowing them to balance the demands of work and anywhere every day using tablets, smart phones, and laptops. Several studies confirmed the disadvantage of using portable devices to include that the communication is interruptible (Chithambo, 2011, 2015; Bhagoliwal & Karjee, 2016; Manworren et al., 2016). Portable devices get lost, stolen, or destroyed, leaving individuals and company information subject to exposure. Breaching of security to technologies connected to mobile devices is much easier to accomplish as compared to those connected to non-mobile devices (Bromwich & Bromwich, 2016; Chithambo, 2011, 2015).

Data security is vital in electronically mediated work because the communication is based on open networks (Friedman & Hoffman, 2008). Earlier studies, Whipple, Allgood, and Larue (2012), show that portable devices continue to pose vulnerability in the health care industry as discovered through one survey where third-year medical students completed a survey related to privacy and security issues concerning mobile devices. According to the results, 67 third-year medical students at a Midwestern university admitted their use of mobile devices and knowledge of how to protect information available through mobile devices. In an effort to gauge participants' concerns over privacy and information security, the survey determined that the most used features of mobile devices were . . . voice-to-voice (100%), text messaging (SMS; 94%), Internet (76.9%), and email (69.3%). As for security, locking of one's personal mobile phone, 54.1% never physically lock their phone, and 58% never electronically locked their personal PDA. The study also showed concerns including emailing patient information intact (66.7%), and posting de-identified information on YouTube (45.2%) or Facebook (42.2%). (Whipple et al., 2012, para. 4)

As discussed by Chithambo (2011, 2015), this is evidence that with the increase in the use of mobile devices, there is a great need for more education and training on privacy and security risks posed with mobile devices. Leaders are encouraged to embrace the mobile technology. Additionally, leaders are encouraged to ensure that telecommuting technology devices used by individuals while away from home are well protected and that the individuals are informed of all matters related to information security.

Historical Overview and Review of the Literature

According to Chithambo (2011, 2015), the history of remote work starts as far back as the 1870s (Abdel-Wahab, 2007; Allen, Golden, & Shockley, 2015) with research showing that remote work was done during World War II, with telephones and satellite as a means of communication. This research starts the historical overview from 1978. The web services industry developed tremendously since 2000, from the use of mobile devices to communicate; with the extensive use of mobile technology, telecommuting has increased (Chithambo, 2011, 2015). Advancement in technology contributed to affordable rates, and thus, working away from the office as a telecommuter has become increasingly available to many workers around the world (Allen, Golden, & Shockley, 2015). The estimated number of telecommuters in 1998 was 15.7 million and the number of telecommuters in 1999 was 19.6 million. The growth rate of mobile technology keeps increasing, remote work continues to rise as companies continue to adapt and allow more individuals to work from home. Currently, almost two decades later, approximately 45% of people in the United States work from home, with the ability to reach many rural areas of third world countries (Ashraf, 2015; Betjeman, Soghoian, & Foran, 2013); contributing to the rate of more than half of the individuals in the world using mobile technology as compared to 30 years ago (Chithambo, 2011, 2015).

Information Privacy and Security Concerns

According to Chithambo (2011, 2015), more information is on the web and individuals communicate at a fast pace, costing companies billions of dollars when data breaches occur. Many companies exchange business online, requiring customers to disclose private information. Customers are reluctant to display information online because of concerns about privacy (Gaurav, Fatemeh, & David, 2015). Among the challenges of eliminating a cyber-attack while operating business is that companies cannot simply shut down a business to eliminate a cyber-attack. Hackers have found a way into the company systems attacking with same malware, even after the 2013 Target attacks on retails stores continue. The Internet was developed with the intentions of honest users but some users take advantage and abuse the opportunity to spam, malware, hacking, phishing, denial of service attacks, click fraud, invasion of privacy, defamation, frauds and violation of digital property rights (Kedgley, 2015). According to Sullivan (2014), in the late 2013, the direct cost in credit card payments estimated to 6.1 billion in 2012. Data breaches increased as the use of mobile devices increased. People can work from anywhere, many of whom work from home part- or full-time, and individuals can access information from anywhere as long as they have a mobile device (Chithambo, 2011; Messenger & Gschwind, 2016), but portable devices can easily be lost or stolen (Bhagoliwal & Karjee, 2016). Corporate assets are more at risk of information breaches, subjecting the organizations to financial and legal risks battles.

The Growth of Remote Work and Benefits to Individuals and Companies

According to several authors, both individuals and companies benefit from telecommuting (Ellison, 2012; Golden & Shockley, 2015; Madlock, 2012, 2013). The benefits to individuals include avoiding the daily commute to a local office and the flexible work schedule, employee work location. Organizations increasingly introduce workplace flexibility practices that provide flexibility with regard to where or when the employee works, the flexibility of not rising up early in the morning to join the morning hassle (Chithambo, 2015; Coenen & Kok, 2014). The increase in telecommuting has benefited many individuals who otherwise would not be able to travel to work (Fink, Dillion, & Wedding, 2015). Most research confirmed that mobile devices contributed to flexible work schedules and places people can work from anywhere any time (Brice, Millicent, & Norris, 2011; Dahlstrom, 2013; Tuncay, 2012).

Company and individual benefits and concerns. Chithambo (2011, 2015) discussed an increase in job satisfaction because of less pressure (such as office meeting attendance), cited most often in literature as a benefit of the use of working away from home (Bloom, Liang, Roberts, & Ying, 2015; Tuncay, 2012). This is also evidenced by an earlier 5-year study discussed by Butler, Aasheim, and Williams (2007), where call center telecommuters of American Water Company worked about 3.98 more hours per month than the traditional office workers between 1998 and 2003 and still seemed satisfied with telecommuting. Individuals can also work in many desired positions of their profession for a number of employers simultaneously (Major et al., 2008; Mello, 2007), and employers reduce operating costs due to less office space for rent and utilities. According to Potter (2003) in an American Community Survey, travel time and expense decreased. The survey showed that on average telecommuters spend 57.6 minutes per day, which can be used for working. Environmentalists are able to benefit from the decrease in number of automobiles on the roads, as it results in a decrease in pollution and oil consumption. As discussed by Chithambo, 2011, the decrease in number of automobiles could also result in a decreased potential for accidents and increased ability to hire special-needs employees. However, having individuals access private company information has also contributed to the increase in data breaches confirms (Bekkers, & Thaens, 2015; Elmaghraby, & Losavio, 2014).

Considerations for characteristics of telecommuters. Chithambo (2011, 2015) stressed that when considering the option of distributing portable devices, work away from home corporations should consider an individual's concentration capacity and an individual's knowledge in information security and privacy. Some workers are better apt with the ability to concentrate on work activities while away from the local office, while others struggle. According to Harrison, Svetieva, and Vishwahath (2016), some individuals have little or no knowledge in how to protect their own online privacy. The traits on telecommuting and online knowledge are not all conducive to effective telecommuting, and do account for the factors involved when companies make the telecommuting decisions which could contribute to data breaches (Chithambo, 2011, 2015). The future workforce will continue doing business in remote locations because both the employee and the company benefit. The need for the traditional office setting continues to decline as mobile technologically increases, resulting in a parallel increase in the number of remote workers.

The rise of telecommuting. According to the report by International Telecommunication, 3.2 billion people would be online, that estimates more than half of the world. Chithambo (2011, 2015) stressed that the future workforce will continue business in remote locations because both the employee and the company benefit (Mamaghani, 2006). The number of telecommuters increased from 4 million in 1995 to 23.6 million in 2000 nationally in the United States, and to over 137 million worldwide, according to Mamaghani's 2006 reports. According to Work Place (2015), the number of remote workers estimated to have increased from 25% in 2011 to 37% in 2015. The need for the traditional office setting continues to decline as mobile technologically increases, resulting in a parallel increase in the number of remote workers (Chithambo, 2011, 2015; Culnan et al., 2008).

Leadership's Role in Information Security Training

Chithambo (2011, 2015) and Culnan and colleagues (2008) confirmed findings that measured attitude and behavior between trained and untrained employees and the results show current similar trends. The implication of themes that emerged remain the same. The emerged themes as described in the next section confirm the existence of the trend in information privacy (Chithambo, 2011, 2015). Fourteen themes emerged as a result of the initial coding process, as illustrated in Table 1.

TABLE 1. THEMES IN INFORMATION SECURITY

1. ID/Passwords	8. Selective
2. Access level	9. Security levels
3. Access on needs basis	10. Protect data
4. Tracking	11. Accountability
5. Access Control	12. Security layers
6. High level structure	13. Frequent software updates
7. Levels, i.e. servers	14. Differentiate access level

Implications of Themes

The streamlined themes below remain the main focus for leadership training and improvement.

- **Theme 1:** Organizations will require security training for telecommuters to make them accountable for information compromise.

- **Theme 2:** The major means of information protection will go beyond the use of data encryption, user IDs, and passwords.

- **Theme 3:** Telecommuters must be allowed to view the information; no printing will be available.

- **Theme 4:** Leaders will enforce management to be accountable for individuals chosen to telecommute.

- **Theme 5:** Information security leaders will enforce the practice of assigning telecommuting access through levels, assigned based on individual needs for information.

- **Theme 6:** Leaders will make sure that there is proper control of the physical protection of company data.

- **Theme 7:** Leaders will make sure that companies have proper control and formal procedures and criteria as to who/when/how to request remote access

Recommendations for Action

Good leadership is important, stresses Madlock (2012), and training individuals in how to properly protect company information is vital, confirms Miller and Tucker (2011). Constant supervision and feedback helps improve and encourage employees learn and improve processes. Information Technology leaders are encouraged to require and enforce security training for teleworkers and make them accountable when information is compromised. The major means of information protection will go beyond the use data encryption, user IDs, and passwords. Rules for all individuals allowed to view company information when working away from the local office must be consistent across the organization. Rules to disallow individuals to print company information when working away from the local office must be consistent across the organization. Information security leaders must enforce strict selection and decision criteria for managers identifying for permitting teleworkers (Chithambo, 2011).

The Researcher's Reflections and Conclusion

According to Chithambo (2011, 2015), diversity existed in the responses to questions on information technology leaders' perception on how telecommuting individuals protect individual and company information. More than 90% of all the participants agreed that employee education and training relative to telecommuting increases the chances of securing company data and decreases the risk of accessing unauthorized information. Training contributes to effective protection of company data, and most participants had a positive perception of the importance of information security training. Some participants were apprehensive about the complexity of information security because information technology continues to change. The information security rules and procedures must keep up with this change.

Because the research study was based on the importance of rules and procedures in information security related to telecommuters, some disagreements arose about what causes the failure for leaders to enforce the rules that are in place to protect proprietary information. The various perceptions included the following: (a) management is responsible for making sure employees are following up with the password changes, (b) the information security management must make sure that there is a mechanism in place that will force employees out of the system if the employee has been using the same password for up to 3 months, and (c) lack of training in information security will cause employees not to apply the required tasks into the system that would help protect unauthorized use of data.

The research study disclosed effective means of securing data when individuals telecommute. In information technology, telecommuting is among the most used means of commuting within the organization without individuals working in the local office. The results and conclusion of this study provides a means through which participants and their experiences in information security create a path to connect with the participants' experiences and to assess any preconceptions and judgments regarding interpretation. During the research study, the researcher prevented biased judgments by narrating only from the participants' experiences. Information technology leaders can use the disclosed information to pioneer and enforce procedures and rules to protect company information when individuals telecommute.

The information disclosed in this study could enable all information technology leaders to use information security procedures to the fullest and best of their ability to provide consistency in the information security rules within their organizations. The importance of this study includes gaining an understanding of the status of the use of information security rules and procedures in all industries. The options discovered during the study could help the information security leaders within the telecommuting community and all other industries.

This study adds to the existing literature in several ways. The study is the first qualitative descriptive study to examine information security policies and procedures in relation to the telecommuting community. Most of the literature reviewed discussed information security with little emphasis in the importance of information security when individuals telecommute. The research has added to the body of knowledge pertaining to the importance of information technology security and the importance of information security awareness in telecommuting. The results of the findings explain, predict, and improve information security policy and procedures to protect company and individual information when individuals work remotely using mobile devices (Chithambo, 2011, 2015).

Leadership's Role in Information Security Training and Privacy

According to Chithambo (2011, 2015), Culnan et al. (2008), and Overby (2013), employer-sponsored training programs on information security awareness have improved teleworkers' perspective in individual and company security awareness and this is a cybersecurity challenge (Roche, Roche, Blaine, & McCreary, 2014). Culnan et al. confirmed findings that measured attitude and behavior between trained and untrained employees. The data gathered from the study and shared earlier illustrates how concentration on access levels has a huge impact in information protection.

Conclusion

Chithambo (2011, 2015) stressed the importance of leaders to understand the fundamental challenges of organizations' ability to prepare and equip security management on cyber-attacks. Effective leaders who understand the key process in how to protect company information are well equipped and respond successfully when the cyber-attack occur. Preparation is integral to prevent or lessen the effects of cyber-attacks. Constant monitoring of information entering and exiting through the organization's portal and rigorous training on information security and privacy will assist leaders and information security management teams resolve and reduce the negative consequences. Cybersecurity is on the rise (Seebruck, 2015) hacker attacks are sophisticated, with recent targets being large e-commerce businesses whose online security has been compromised (Manworren, et al., 2015). Chithambo (2011, 2015) stresses that cyber-attacks are on the rise. Web users keep increasing, and thus cybersecurity training is crucial. The physical connection among individuals and companies, which would take days to connect, has now been replaced by virtual connections that can occur in just seconds. Web connectedness is on the rise and has become a way of doing business and conducting individual social meetings. Some online users make good use of web access, while others see the opportunity to steal and exploit others. Cyber-attacks affect organizations economically. Individual privacy is at stake and individual lives are in danger when hackers attack for various reasons. Online users range from little to no knowledge in how to protect information from hackers, thus training individual users in how to protect private information would in part reduce hack attacks. Companies are obligated to set, train, and follow-up on policy on how to protect business information from hackers.

THOUGHTS FROM THE ACADEMIC ENTREPRENEUR

The problem to be solved:

- Developing appropriate training programs on information security specific to each organization. Keep up with the fast changing technology and the complexity of cyber hackers.

The goals:

- Explore literature to determine a need for further research on barriers to promotion in information technology in relation to gender biases, and generational differences.

- Explore innovative mentoring practices designed to increase cybersecurity individuals representing minority in executive positions.

The questions to ask:

- Is there persistent underrepresentation of a variety of administrative and executive positions in all occupational industries in the 21st century?

- Is there persistent underrepresentation of minority in information technology industry because of organizational culture?

- Does persistent underrepresentation of minority in the information technology industry link to a lack of motivation and experience, generational differences, ethnicity, same gender partiality, or self-preservation?

- What is the effect of mentoring programs on gender biases, stereotyping, organizational culture, and upward mobility for minority in the information technology industry in the 21st century?

- What are the implications of implementing systemic mentoring programs regardless of gender differences and ethnicity in the information technology industry?

- How would refractive thinking strategies impact perceived barriers to minority promotion in the information technology industry?

Today's business application:

- Understanding innovative mentoring practices and programs that may reduce perceived biases and barriers for minority seeking executive information technology positions.
- Empowering minority to prepare for information technology leadership roles by participating in mentoring programs.
- Empowering leaders with research data on the importance of intentional mentoring programs for minority in the information technology industry.

REFERENCES

Abdel-Wahab, A. (2007). Employees' attitudes towards telecommuting. An empirical investigation in the Egyptian Governorate of Dakahlia. *Behaviour & Information Technology, 26*, 367–375. doi:10.1080/01449290500535426

Allen, T. D., Golden, T. D., & Shockley, K. M. (2015). How effective is telecommuting? Assessing the status of our scientific findings. *Psychological Science in the Public Interest, 16*(2). doi:10.1177/1529100615593273

Ashraf, M. (2015). A development impact assessment on the use of ICT (Mobile Phone) in rural areas of Bangladesh. *International Journal of Information Communication Technologies and Human Development (IJICTHD), 7*(1). doi:10.4018/IJICTHD.2015010101

Bhagoliwal, S., & Karjee, J. (2016). Securing data using cryptography. *International Journal of Advanced Networking and Applications, 7*, 2925–2930. doi:10.5121/ijcnc.2013.5310

Betjeman, T. J., Soghoian, S. E., & Foran, M. P. (2013). mHealth in Sub-Saharan Africa. *International Journal of Telemedicine and Applications, 2013*(6). doi:10.1155/2013/482324

Blanke, S., & McGrady, E. (2016). When it comes to securing patient health information for breaches, your best medicine. *Journal of Healthcare Risk Management, 36*(1). doi:10.1002/jhrm.21230

Bloom, N., Liang, J., Roberts, J., & Ying, Z. J. (2015). Does working from home work? Evidence from a Chinese Experiment. *The Quarterly Journal of Economics, 130*(1). Retrieved from http://www.nber.org/papers/w18871

Bromwich, M., & Bromwich, R. (2016). Privacy risks when using mobile devices in health care. *Canadian Medical Association Journal, 188*(12). doi:10.1503 /cmaj.160026

Chithambo, L. (2011). *Security concerns in telecommuting within the information technology industry* (Doctoral dissertation). Retrieved from ProQuest Dissertations & Theses Full Text database. (UMI No. 3574919)

Chithambo, L. (2015). Security concerns in telecommuting within the information technology industry. *A Journal of the Academic Forum, 4*(2), 67–78. Retrieved from http://www.theacademicforum.org/

Coenen, M., & Kok, R. A. W. (2014). Workplace flexibility and new product development performance: The role of telework and flexible work schedules. *European Management Journal, 32*(4). doi:10.1016/j.emj.2013.12.003

Culnan, M., Foxman, E., & Ray, A. (2008). Why IT executives should help employees secure their home computers. *MIS Quarterly Executive, 7*(1), 49–56. Retrieved from http://misqe.org/ojs2/index.php/misqe

Dahlstrom, T. R. (2013). Telecommuting and Leadership Style. *Public Personnel Management, 42*(3). doi:10.1177/0091026013495731

Elmaghraby, A. S., & Losavio, M. M. (2014). Cybersecurity challenges in smart cities: safety, security, and privacy. *Journal of Advanced Research, 5*(4). doi:10.1016/j.jare.2014.02.006

Fink, L. S., Dillion, A., & Wedding D. K. (2015). The Americans with disabilities act, telecommuting and reasonable accommodation. *Journal of Accountability Leadership and Ethics, 12,* 491–497. Retrieved from http://www.academia.edu

Friedman, J., & Hoffman, D. (2008). Protecting data on mobile devices: A taxonomy of security threats to mobile computing and review of applicable defenses. *Information Knowledge Systems Management, 7*(1/2), 159–180. Retrieved from http://dl.acm.org/citation.cfm?id=1402714

Gaurav, B., Fatemeh, M. Z., & David, G. (2015). Do context and personality matter?: Trust and privacy concerns in disclosing private information online. *Information & Management, 53*(1). doi:10.1016/j.im.2015.08.001

Harrison, B., Svetieva, E., & Vishwahath, A. (2016) Individual processing of phishing emails: how attention and elaboration protect against phishing. *Online Information Review, 40*(2). http://dx.doi.org/10.1108/OIR-04-2015-0106

Kantor, D. (2014). Broken payment system assures another data breach like Target's. *Credit Union Journal, 18*(3). Retrieved from https://www.cujournal.com

Liao, Q., & Zhen, L. (2014). Portfolio optimization or computer and mobile botnets. *International Journal of Information Security, 13*(1). doi:10.1007/s10207-013-0206-9

Madlock, P. E. (2012). The influence of supervisors' leadership style on telecommuters. *Journal of Business Strategies, 29*(1). Retrieved from http://cdm2635-01.cdmhost.com/cdm/search/collection/p263501coll9

Madlock, P. E. (2013). The influence of motivational language in the technologically mediated realm of telecommuters. *Human Resource Management Journal, 23*(2). doi:10.1111/j.1748-8583.2012.00191.x

Major, D., Verive, J., & Joice, W. (2008). Telework as a dependent care solution: Examining current practice to improve telework management strategies. *Psychologist-Manager Journal, 11*(1), 65–91. doi:10.1080/10887150801967134

Manworren, N., Letwat, J., & Daily, O. (2016). Why you should care about the Target data breach. *Business Horizons, May.* doi:10.1016/j.bushor.2016.01.002

Messenger, J. C., & Gschwind, L. (2016). Three generations of Telework: New ICTs and the revolution from home office to virtual office. *New Technology, Work, and Employment, 31*(3), 195–208. doi:10.1111/ntwe.12073

Miller, A. R., & Tucker, C. E. (2011). The encryption of customer data. *Journal of Policy Analysis and Management, 30*(3). doi:10.1002/pam.20590

Musheer, A., & Sheeraz, A. (2014). Transformation of smart phone to super phone: A future oriented gadget. *The Journal of Management Awareness, 17*(2). doi:10.5958/0974-0945.2014.00001.6

Nofer, M., Hinz, O., Muntermann, J., & Rossnagel, H. (2014). The economic impact of privacy violations and security breaches. *A Laboratory Experiment. Business & Information Systems Engineering, 6,* 339–348. doi:10.1007/s12599-014-0351-3

Seebruck, R. (2015). A typology of hackers. *Digital Investigation, 14,* A1-A2, 1–76. doi:10.1016/j.diin.2015.07.002

Suarez-Tangil, G., Tapiador, J. E., Lombardi, F., & Di Pietro, R. (2014). Thwarting obfuscated malware via different fault analysis. *Computer, 47*(6). doi:10.1109/MC.2014.169

Whipple, E. C., Allgood, K. L., & LaRue, K. M. (2012). Third-year medical students' knowledge of security and privacy issues concerning mobile devices. *Medical teacher, 34*(8), e532-e548. doi:10.3109/0142159X.2012.670319

About the Author...

Dr. Loyce Chithambo resides in the Dallas Metroplex area of Texas. Dr. Loyce holds several accredited degrees, including a Bachelor of Science (BS) in Computer Science from Bluefield State College West Virginia; a Master of Information Systems (MIS) from City University Seattle, and a Doctorate of Management (DM) in Information Systems from the University of Phoenix. Dr. Loyce works as a consultant in the Information Technology Industry and has worked for several Fortune 500 Companies.

Dr. Loyce is a Faculty Member at the University of Phoenix, approved to teach Information Technology / Systems courses. She is also a Content Area Expert in Information Technology Doctoral Research Studies at Grand Canyon University. Dr. Loyce is passionate about academia and with a passion to remain current with the ever changing technological needs. She is also a member of Project Management Institute (PMI).

Her doctoral study, *Information Security Protection in the Telecommuting Industry,* provided her the opportunity to gain academic and working experience.

To reach Dr. Loyce, please e-mail: smithloyce@ymail.com. Also visit www.linkedin.com/in/dr-loyce-chithambo-dm-ist-1006a011

CHAPTER 6

The Healthcare Cybersecurity Challenge

Dr. James Rice

During 2016, the United States healthcare industry organizations reported 27, 314,647 security breaches (Lord, 2017). According to the Department of Health and Human Services (2017), the top five U.S. healthcare security breaches affected more than 109.2 million individuals in 2016 (as cited in Modern Healthcare, 2017). Furthermore, the Identity Theft Resource Center (2017) reported that data breaches increased significantly year-over-year. Healthcare industry data loss represented one-third of U.S. data breaches in 2016.

Large numbers can cause anyone to lose interest and consider the topic to be ordinary, routine, or someone else's problem. However, Johnson and Johnson reported that their insulin infusion pump was vulnerable and could be hacked resulting in overdosing the patient wearing the device, possibly even patient death (Finkle, 2016; Reuters, 2016). Healthcare cybersecurity is about more than regulatory compliance or identity theft. A cybersecurity failure in healthcare can mean that someone dies. Healthcare professionals must think about cybersecurity as more than technical controls and processes; healthcare cybersecurity is responsible for the health and safety of patients. A goal of this paper is to explore issues and cybersecurity concerns unique to healthcare and provide a perspective that many healthcare cybersecurity professionals have not considered.

The Healthcare Cybersecurity Challenge

Many cybersecurity professionals consider it their primary responsibility to identify security vulnerabilities and regulatory compliance gaps in their organization (Doarn & Merrell, 2015; Lord, 2017). Cybersecurity professionals implement technical, physical, and administrative controls to reduce business risk. Because new vulnerabilities and threats emerge daily, cybersecurity professionals must remain vigilant for security weaknesses and breaches that expose nonpublic information, intellectual property, damage business processes, or interrupt customer services.

Most cyber threat protection technologies and techniques are the same across industries and types of business; However, healthcare is unique in the level of risk to individual health and safety. The following sections include the motivations of the various *bad actors* threatening the healthcare industry. Subsequent sections will provide an overview of unique healthcare business drivers that cybersecurity professionals must pay special attention to. The challenge for healthcare cybersecurity professionals is more than protecting the risk to the business financials and reputation. The job is about protecting the life of patients that the organization serves (Perakslis, 2014; Vaas, 2016; Wellington, 2014).

Philosophical Framework for Cybersecurity Evaluation

Some individuals suggest that cybersecurity has a universal meaning regardless of the context (Bradley, 2013;

Finnemore & Hollis, 2016; Information Systems Audit and Control Association [ISACA], 2017). That is, the phrase is a description of a set of technologies and practices that secure an asset for the organization. This definition of cybersecurity remains consistent with the *semantic theory of meaning*. The semantic theory of meaning supports the assertion that facts, truth, or virtues of the subject define the word or phrase (Speaks, 2017).

A more general *semantic theory* includes the concept of *referential deference* (Katz & Fodor, 1963; Speaks, 2017). This more general application the theories related to natural language and meaning enables a word or phrase to have meaning that is adaptable to its context or frame of reference. The concept of *referential deference* is the framework used to explore cybersecurity for healthcare organizations. Specifically, how does the healthcare industry context alter or enrich the understanding of cybersecurity motivations, technologies, practices, and disciplines?

Healthcare Cybersecurity is Unique

Consumers seldom think about healthcare organizations as a target for hackers (Coronado & Wong, 2014; Lord, 2017; Prater, 2014). Unlike a bank, health care providers seldom retain patient financial information. Cybersecurity and data privacy is a less significant concern to many patients than either the cost, quality, or availability of patient care. Because of this outcome-driven focus, traditionally health care organizations prioritized investment in medical care capability and placed less emphasis on investment in cybersecurity (Papoutsi et al., 2015; Prater, 2014).

Many health care organizations and consumers do not consider the threat that cyber criminals can pose to patient health and safety (Gardner, 2012; Thimbleby, 2017). However, it is difficult to recover quickly from the loss to cyber criminals because of the persistent nature of data. A fingerprint is a fingerprint for life. If a cyber terrorist gains access to or control of a patient medical device, modify the data, or change the device configuration to harm or even kill the patient. cyber criminals are attracted to healthcare industry data and information services because of their unique nature (Coronado & Wong, 2014; HealthITSecurity, 2015; Messmer, 2013; Miliard, 2015).

When preparing to examine cybersecurity for the healthcare industry, healthcare professionals must start by surveying key elements of the healthcare cyber-threat landscape. These elements include attributes of the individuals who threaten the security of the information systems used for healthcare delivery. Cybersecurity professionals must also understand what is unique about healthcare information systems that attract *bad actors*. The next section includes an exploration of this landscape in more detail.

Healthcare Cybersecurity Landscape

When exploring the healthcare cybersecurity landscape, it is helpful to start with what attracts bad actors to the industry's assets. *Motivation* to breach a medical organization's security is a useful way to group the bad actors. For this reason, *motivation* categories will include entertainment, ideology, financial gain, and incitement of terror. I will refer to bad actors as *casual hackers, cyber ideologists, cyber criminals,* and *cyber terrorists* (Lakhani & Wolf, 2003; Myers, Powers, & Faissol, 2009; White Hat Security, 2017).

The casual hacker is an individual or small group of people who seek to penetrate the security of an organization for personal convenience or to see if it is possible (Currys, 2011). The phrase, "I hacked it because I could" is a good way to think about these individuals. They seek a challenge and a way to test their skills. In general, casual hackers lack interest in notoriety or in doing damage. Personal satisfaction is the best way to understand their motivation (Reiss, 2004; Shaw, Sachs, Parker, Devost, & Sachs, 2004). For example, a teenager who hacks a parent's infusion pump in the hospital room, so he or she does not have to walk across the room to read the display, is a casual hacker.

Cyber ideologists seek to make a point, support a personal point-of-view, or promote a political position through their hacking efforts (Shaw et al., 2004). The phrase, "See, I told you so" is a reasonable way to understand the motivation of this type of cybersecurity threat. Gaining access to private data, nonpublic information, corrupting the capability of the organization, or seeking to gain an advantage over competition are all examples of cyber ideologist activities; However, support of an ideology limits his or her efforts. He or she will stop before doing intentional or significant damage to the organization (Federico, Deason, & Fisher, 2012; Lakhani & Wolf, 2003). No evidence is available to indicate that this form of cybersecurity risk is more-or-less significant for healthcare organizations than for businesses in any other industry.

Cyber criminals are individuals who seek to collect nonpublic information or disrupt information services for personal gain (Espenson, 2017; Fuentes, 2017; Reiss, 2004). Theft of Personal Health Information (PHI) enables identity theft, and the number of theft is growing as the value of an electronic health record increases. Ransomware, blocking access to critical information until the healthcare organization pays a ransom, is on the rise across all industries

(DeNisco, 2016). Cyber-crime is new to most healthcare organizations. In response to legislation and regulation, the industry has experienced significant merger and acquisition activity to achieve efficiency that results from economy-of-scale. Unfortunately, evaluation of security technology or the cybersecurity program is frequently not a part of healthcare merger activity. Thus, economy-of-scale has also offered cyber criminals with an increasingly valuable asset to target, and they are taking advantage of it (Kusserow, 2013; Landi, 2016; Socas, 2015). Cyber criminals do not seek notoriety because the value of the stolen healthcare data degrades once the organization is awareness of the theft. Therefore, the goal of cyber criminals is to breach an environment, steal information, and leave without detection or notoriety. Then use that information for personal gain.

Anger, frustration, or ideology motivate the cyber terrorist. Their goal is to erode trust and confidence in an institution or government (Harries & Yellowlees, 2013; Jain, Gyanchandani, & Khare, 2016; Tafya, 2011). When hospitals were small, and patient care was not technology dependent, the opportunity for cyber terrorists is minimal. However, as an increasing number of medical devices are network-connected, and the number of U.S. healthcare organization has decreased through merger-and-acquisition, the healthcare industry is a more attractive target for cyber terrorists (Levine, 2017; Nash, McGregor, & Prentice, 2011). The ability of cyber terrorists to exploit security weaknesses in medical devices, both external and implantable, resulting in the alteration of data or delivery of inappropriate treatment that can kill a patient is very real. Harming a significant number of patients, killing a public figure, or holding a patient's life for ransom are potential targets for cyber terrorists (Alqahtani, 2015).

The Healthcare Cybersecurity Challenge

As a refractive thinker, grounding exploration of healthcare security in these foundational business activities can free healthcare professionals to see security and safety through a new lens. Building on the knowledge of what motivates bad actors in the healthcare landscape, the next step is to examine business events that draw the attention of these individuals. For our examination, a good way to remember the key activities are the three R's—Regulation, Records, and Reporting. (see Figure 1).

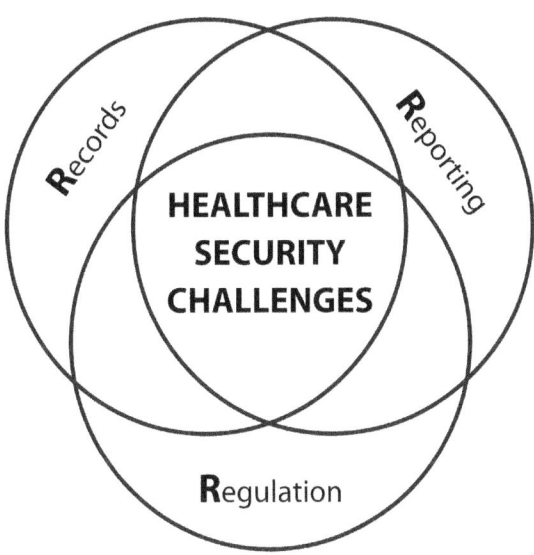

Figure 1: Healthcare Security Challenges—The Three 'R's

Nearly every U.S. president, since Lyndon B. Johnson signed Medicare and Medicaid in 1964, introduced legislation to enhance access to medical care and improve patient safety (Centers for Medicare and Medicaid Services, 2013; Scott, Ruef, Mendel, & Caronna, 2000). Under President

Barack Obama, *The Patient Protection and Affordable Care Act* (2010) and *The American Recovery and Reinvestment Act (ARRA), Title XIII* (2009) introduced significant changes to the patient healthcare access and structural changes healthcare organizations. The goal of the most recent legislation include further improvements the quality of patient outcomes and enhance the privacy of patient data (Harrington, 2010). Given the trajectory of healthcare regulation, continued development of market regulations is a reasonable assumption.

Healthcare organizations are not new to audits. In addition to regular license reviews and facilities assessments, both payers and providers participate in the following reviews and audits (Busch, 2012; Crump, 2015):

- Risk Adjustment and Medical Record Reviews (MRRs)
- Medicare Advantage Risk Adjustment Data Validation (RADV)
- Health Effectiveness Data and Information Set (HEDIS)
- Diagnosis Related Group (DRG) payment integrity reviews
- Care and quality improvement audits
- Five-Star program audits.

Since the passage of the ARRA (2009), the Department of Health and Human Services (HHS) and the Office of Civil Rights (OCR) continue to increase inspection of information systems within healthcare organizations. The number and complexity of technology and data privacy controls have resulted in increasing investment in governance, risk, and compliance software to manage regulatory compliance.

Healthcare Provider Mergers and Acquisitions

The Patient Protection and Affordable Care Act (2010) and the American Recovery and Reinvestment Act (2009) are U.S. federal legislation that affects healthcare organizations. Both legislative efforts, directly and indirectly, the funding of healthcare organizations. As businesses funding changes, organizational structure and governance models evolved to maintain financial viability (S&P Dow Jones, 2013). In response, healthcare organizations continue to restructure and, since 2009, the rate of the healthcare industry mergers and acquisitions includes a significant increase (Block, 2013; Blumenthal, 2011; Kusserow, 2013; Pricewaterhouse Coopers LLP, 2013). In 2015, Becker's Hospital Review reported 637 United States health care system mergers in 2013 and 752 transactions in 2014, an 18% increase in healthcare merger and acquisition activity. In January of 2017, Becker's Hospital Review reported a 55% growth in hospital merger and acquisition activity over the preceding 6-year period (Ellison, 2017). Merger activity is one indication that healthcare executives continue to look for business efficiency and economies of scale to respond to the significant changes in the regulatory environment (Adamopoulos, 2013; Birk, 2010; McGlynn, 2008; Silow-Carroll, Edwards, & Rodin, 2012).

A benefit of a smaller number of healthcare providers in the United States is the potential for economy of scale and a reduced cost of operation. However, a security challenge resulting from a smaller number of large organizations is the volume of information put at risk when a successful breach occurs (HIPAA Journal, 2017; U.S. Department of Health & Human Services, 2017). Maintaining and auditing technical, physical, and administrative security controls when merging organizations is difficult (Evans, 2013). Healthcare cybersecurity professionals have reported that the challenges associated with maintaining a strong security posture are significant. A contributing factor is the growing number of industry mergers and acquisitions. Knowing this reality, hackers, cyber criminals, and cyber terrorists may, justifiably, consider healthcare organizations attractive targets.

Healthcare organizations are beginning to adopt a series of premerger safeguards to minimize the organizational financial impact and risk to patient safety. These safeguards apply to both the acquiring entity and the purchased entity (Betbeze, 2013; Ray & Gallaher, 2015). These safeguards include:

- Appointment of a Chief Information Security Officer (CISO)

- Establishment or review of incident response team capabilities

- Review of data classifications and refresh data protection methods

- Creation of organizational level identity and access management

- Implementation of security awareness training

- Cybersecurity insurance

- Board level reporting of the organization's risk posture.

Even though of these practices may exist in healthcare payer networks, they are new to many healthcare provider organizations. Each practice helps ensure a merger or acquisition does not result in financial damage to the business.

Furthermore, these practices also improve the cybersecurity of the business (Kusserow, 2013). Refractive thinkers integrate their knowledge of the cybersecurity threats to the business and potential patient risks when developing these practices.

Remote Patient Care and Biometric Data Collection

In the United States, network attached medical devices enable the collection of patient biometric data and sending alerts about critical conditions to medical professionals–sometimes even before the patient knows there is an issue exists (Aqeel ur Rehman, Khan, & Rehman, 2017). Hospital rooms and care facilities include a variety of network-connected medical devices. Also, network attached medical devices provide remote monitoring and treatment of patients, enabling telemedicine (Doarn & Merrell, 2015). Medically implanted devices are connected to networks to simplify patient care access and enhance the patient's quality of life. Network-connected devices enable medical professionals to deliver critical care without the need to be in the same location as the patient (Harries & Yellowlees, 2013). The growing number of network-connected medical devices has made it possible for patient care options to geographically remote patients. These options enable access to care that was not previously possible. Secure healthcare data collection and management is coming to the forefront of healthcare cybersecurity since the Internet of Things (IoT) entered the dialogue of medical security professionals (Stolpe, 2016; Tulasidas, Mackay, Hudson, & Balachandran, 2017).

New medical device innovations can lead to new patient security and safety threats. Connecting an infusion pump, a pacemaker, or other medical devices to a network exposes the device to cyber criminals and cyber terrorists. For example, in 2016, as many as 2 million infusion pumps were in use in the United States to deliver fluids and medications to patients in controlled amounts. By gaining privileged access to legacy medical devices through the network, cyber criminals and cyber terrorists may access patient data or compromise the care of the patient. Because of the rigorous testing requirements, security testing and patching of medical devices is a slow and expensive process (Fu & Blum, 2014; Miliard, 2015). At the end of 2016, as many as one-third of medical computers, devices, and modalities were running insecure and even unpatched operating systems (Fuentes, 2017). The result of the significant number of vulnerabilities and pervasive nature of medical devices is the ability of even casual or recreational cyber hackers to succeed in penetrating healthcare networks. These new vulnerabilities provide a target rich environment for cyber criminals and cyber terrorists.

The growing volume of network attached medical devices, combined with the difficulty of updating or patching medical devices, resulted in a challenge for security professionals to keep ahead of known vulnerabilities (Gonsalves, 2013; Wellington, 2014). Medical devices present a unique security challenge because traditional end-point-protection technologies cannot be applied and there are limits to the ability to patch or configure them. Through the application of refractive thinking, cybersecurity professionals are turning to zero-trust network products and practices to secure these sensitive devices and moving beyond traditional end-point-protection practices (Cormier, 2016; eWeek, 2011; Rashid, 2011, 2011). Enhancements to authentication and authorization protocols for implantable medical device security is also the subject of research and collaboration among device manufacturers. The challenge of securing access to these devices is also increasing the focus Identity and Access

Management (IAM) technologies (Camara, Peris-Lopez, & Tapiador, 2015; Halperin, Heydt-Benjamin, Fu, Kohno, & Maisel, 2008).

Electronic Medical Record and Medical Data Analytics

The Affordable Care Act established the Prevention and Public Health Fund to provide expanded and sustained U.S. Federal investments in prevention and public health. The goal of the fund is to enhance health care quality and to improve patient outcomes. The Healthy Places initiative by the Centers for Disease Control (CDC) is a compliment to the Department of Health and Human Services programs. This legislation also compliments community health initiatives by other U.S. Federal agencies (Koplan & Fleming, 2000; Office of Disease Prevention and Health Promotion, 2014). These funds invest in evidence-based activities including research, reporting, public health capability, immunizations, tobacco prevention, and public health training (Department of Health and Human Services, 2015). Evidence of the value of these initiatives is beginning to emerge, such as a reduction in patient re-admittance (Boiey & Proctor, 2015; De Stefano, Rangon, & Lapostolle, 2016; Hagen & Richmond, 2008; Hisham, Ng, Liew, Hamzah, & Ho, 2016).

A goal of the expanding use of the electronic medical record is to enhance the quality of patient medical care and community health (Bartels & Parrish, 2017; Belle et al., 2015). As medical data collection and aggregation continues, the value of medical information to cyber criminals also increases. In 2014, a medical record was worth up to 10 times more than a stolen credit card number. By 2016, as the scope of information aggregation grew, the value of the record increased to more than 80 times that of the credit card number (Compliance, 2016; Humer & Finkle, 2014). The electronic medical record is a significant and growing motivation for both individual and professional cyber criminals. An emerging target for fraudulent intent, political gain, and ideological purposes are the repositories of medical data and sensitive data (Harries & Yellowlees, 2013; Levine, 2017).

The combination of growing healthcare data warehouses, new medical analytics methods, and community health reporting have resulted in security challenges that historically were a lower priority for healthcare cybersecurity professionals. New areas to consider are data classification, data masking, de-identification of information, and data loss prevention. An area to note is a return to the basics of backup, recovery, and disaster recovery planning to protect from the increased threat of ransomware in healthcare (DeNisco, 2016; Ragan, 2009). These techniques and technologies help healthcare organizations and security professional ensure the privacy and security of patient data resulting in lower patient risk.

Healthcare Security: It is About the People

No discussion about healthcare cybersecurity is complete without an exploration of the human element. The security of critical medical information services and the privacy of sensitive patient data require both the skilled services of experienced security professionals and the vigilance of all individuals entrusted with access to these services and data. This section will include a reflection of methods used in healthcare organizations to minimize risks from human factors.

In the United States, healthcare executives remain increasingly aware of the critical nature of security (Coronado &

Wong, 2014). Executives are aware that hiring skilled security professionals is increasingly difficult. The limited availability of security professionals means an increase in salaries and other operating costs that may not be sustainable (Computer Economics, 2013; Coronado & Wong, 2014; Grealish, 2016). Security staff shortages may result in unidentified or failure to remediate gaps in the required administrative, technical, and physical controls used to maintain a compliant and secure health information service capability. Healthcare executives are relying on security consultants and Managed Security Service Providers (MSSP) to fill the gaps. Consultants and managed security services can be a good long-term solution in many cases. However, effective governance is needed to realize the best possible business value of health information systems, including continuous evaluation of the cost, quality, and knowledge management (Chen, Huang, & Hsiao, 2010; Keyes, 2006).

Another key human factor in a healthcare organization security plan are employees who have access to sensitive medical data and information services. These individuals are possibly the single greatest vulnerability these organizations face (Grealish, 2016; Healthcare Security Alert, 2008). Social hacking is increasingly sophisticated and raising the security awareness of employees and contractors is a necessary component of a security program to protect data privacy and reduce patient risk. Employee security awareness is an essential aspect of an organization's security defense and depth planning and often represents a significant culture change for healthcare provider organizations (Grealish, 2016; Thimbleby, 2017). Increasingly, healthcare leaders consider security training is a condition of employment (Knapp & Ferrante, 2012). Employee knowledge is tested through random email phishing and other ethical hacking exercises. Employees who do not comply with company policies have the "opportunity" to refresh their training or face disciplinary actions.

Conclusion

Healthcare cybersecurity has evolved significantly. Beyond compliance with minimum standards established in legislation and regulations, security professionals are emerging as individuals entrusted with managing business risk, data privacy, and patient safety. Healthcare professionals can leverage many of the same technologies and methods used in other industries. Identity and access management, end-point-protection, network security, data classification, encryption, organizational policies, and other security capabilities are not unique to healthcare. However, the unique and very personal nature of the threats to medical data and patient safety result in a potentially different prioritization of limited security resources (Coronado & Wong, 2014). As medical technology continues to evolve and enhance the quality of patient care, security prioritization that will continue to challenge healthcare security professionals to think beyond traditional security solutions to ensure both compliant and safety through the practice of refractive thinking (Lentz, 2010).

THOUGHTS FROM THE ACADEMIC ENTREPRENEUR

The problem:
- Identifying the unique priorities and challenges faced by healthcare cybersecurity professionals

The goal:
- Understanding that healthcare cybersecurity is more than deploying technical controls. Cybersecurity professionals must understand the motivation of bad actors who pose a threat to properly prioritize risk and then protect the lives of patients in addition to the business' assets.

The questions to ask:
- What differentiates a casual hackers, cyber criminals, cyber ideologists, and cyber terrorists?
- Why is personal health information an attractive target for cyber criminals?
- What is the potential implication of a cyber terrorist gaining access to health information systems?
- Why should healthcare cybersecurity professionals and executives care about emerging security practices being developed for the Internet of Things?
- How well are cybersecurity considerations integrated into merger and acquisition strategies of the organization?
- How aware of cybersecurity threats are the employees of the healthcare organization?

Today's Business Application:
- Cybersecurity professionals must know what constitutes healthcare sensitive data, where is it created, how it is stored, and who has legitimate access to minimize security threats.

- Cybersecurity investments must balance both business risk and patient safety by regularly assessing both common security threats and those threats unique to healthcare organizations.
- Security awareness training at all levels of the organization will reduce the risk to the business and minimize threats to patient safety.
- Healthcare executives and cybersecurity professionals who create an organizational culture of information security are more likely to mitigate cyber threats and protect systems, data, and patients.

REFERENCES

Adamopoulos, H. (2013, October 22). Moody's: 5 key for-profit hospital consolidation trends [Trade]. Retrieved from http://www.beckershospitalreview.com

Alqahtani, A. (2015). Towards a framework for the potential cyber-terrorist threat to critical national infrastructure: A quantitative study. *Information and Computer Security; Bingley, 23,* 532–569. https://dx.doi.org/10.1108/ICS-09-2014-0060

Aqeel ur Rehman, Khan, I. U., & Rehman, S. ur. (2017). A review on big data security and privacy in healthcare applications. In F. P. G. Márquez & B. Lev (Eds.), *Big Data Management* (pp. 71–89). Springer International Publishing. https://dx.doi.org/10.1007/978-3-319-45498-6_4

Bartels, A., & Parrish, R. (2017, February 8). US government Sector tech spending trends, 2017 To 2018. *Forester.* Retrieved from https://www.forrester.com

Belle, A., Thiagarajan, R., Soroushmehr, S. M. R., Navidi, F., Beard, D. A., & Najarian, K. (2015). Big data analytics in healthcare. *BioMed Research International; New York, 16.* https://dx.doi.org/10.1155/2015/370194

Betbeze, P. (2013). Despite merger activity, negative credit conditions persist. *Health Governance Report, 23,* 7–8. Retrieved from http://www.hcpro.com/

Birk, S. (2010). Quality cost efficiency: The new quality-cost imperative. *Healthcare Executive, 25,* 14–16, 18–20, 22, 24. Retrieved from http://www.ache.org/

Block, D. (2013). Disruptive innovation: Contributing to a value-based health care system. *Physician Executive, 39,* 46–50, 52. Retrieved from https://www.ncbi.nlm.nih.gov/pubmed/24180188

Blumenthal, R. G. (2011). The next wave of health-care mergers. *Barron's, 91,* 23. Retrieved from http://www.barrons.com/

Boiey, C., & Proctor, R. (2015, March). *Insights at UC Irvine With Hadoop helps reduce patient re-admittance rates and improves patient care.* Industry presented at the HIMSS Virtual Event. Retrieved from http://www.himss.org

Bradley, J. F. (2013, May 5). A first step toward universal cybersecurity standards? [Industry]. Retrieved from https://princelobelblog.com/

Busch, R. S. (2012). *Healthcare fraud: Auditing and detection guide.* Hoboken, NJ: John Wiley & Sons.

Camara, C., Peris-Lopez, P., & Tapiador, J. E. (2015). Security and privacy issues in implantable medical devices: A comprehensive survey. *Journal of Biomedical Informatics, 55,* 272–289. https://dx.doi.org/10.1016/j.jbi.2015.04.007

Centers for Medicare and Medicaid Services. (2013, June 13). History: Centers for Medicare & Medicaid services [Government]. Retrieved from http://www.cms.gov

Chen, C.-J., Huang, J.-W., & Hsiao, C. (2010). Knowledge management and innovativeness: The role of organizational climate and structure. *International Journal of Manpower, 31,* 848–870. https://dx.doi.org/10.1108/01437721011088548

Compliance, C. (2016, May 19). Move over credit cards: Stolen medical records are selling for record prices on the dark web. Retrieved from https://clearwatercompliance.com

Computer Economics. (2013). IT spending and staffing benchmarks 2013/2014: IT budget/cost metrics and other key performance indicators by industry and organization size. Irvine, CA: *Computer Economics.* Retrieved from http://www.computereconomics.com

Cormier, A. (2016, September 21). First micro-segmentation benchmark report validates VMware NSX capabilities enable a zero-trust model. *Business Wire.* New York, NY. Retrieved from http://www.businesswire.com/news/home/20160921005873/en/Micro-Segmentation-Benchmark-Report-Validates-VMware-NSX-Capabilities

Coronado, A. J., & Wong, T. L. (2014). Healthcare cybersecurity risk management: Keys to an effective plan. *Biomedical Instrumentation & Technology, 48,* 26–30. https://dx.doi.org/10.2345/0899-8205-48.s1.26

Crump, D. (2015, February 3). 6 top healthcare audit types. Retrieved from http://www.healthcarefinancenews.com/blog/6-top-healthcare-audit-types

Currys. (2011, August 9). Are you a casual hacker? Retrieved from http://techtalk.currys.co.uk/gadgets/are-you-a-casual-hacker/

De Stefano, C., Rangon, C.-M., & Lapostolle, F. (2016). Plaidoyer pour une recherche qualitative de qualité dans toutes les spécialités. *La Presse Médicale, 45,* 812–813. https://dx.doi.org/10.1016/j.lpm.2016.07.006

DeNisco, A. (2016, September 16). Cybersecurity: Two-thirds of CIOs say threats increasing, cite growth of ransomware [Industry]. Retrieved from http://www.techrepublic.com/article/cybersecurity-two-thirds-of-cios-say-threats-increasing-cite-growth-of-ransomware/

Department of Health and Human Services. (2015, January 2). Prevention and public health fund [Text]. Retrieved from https://www.hhs.gov

Doarn, C. R., & Merrell, R. C. (2015). Accessibility and vulnerability: ensuring security of data in telemedicine. *Telemedicine Journal and E-Health: The Official Journal of the American Telemedicine Association, 21,* 143–144. https://dx.doi.org/10.1089/tmj.2015.9996

Ellison, A. (2017, January 18). Hospital M&A activity jumps 55 percent in 6 years: 5 findings [Industry]. Retrieved from http://www.beckershospital review.com

Espenson, A. (2017, March 13). Cyber-attacks against healthcare companies [Industry]. Retrieved from http://techzulu.com/cyber-attacks-healthcare-companies/

Evans, M. (2013, October 23). Healthcare reform update: ACA will accelerate hospital mergers, Moody's says [Trade]. Retrieved November 28, 2013, from http://www.modernhealthcare.com

eWeek. (2011). Making the case for zero-trust security. *Author, 28,* 35–35. Retrieved from http://www.eweek.com

Federico, C. M., Deason, G., & Fisher, E. L. (2012). Ideological asymmetry in the relationship between epistemic motivation and political attitudes. *Journal of Personality and Social Psychology: Attitudes and Social Cognition, 103,* 381–398. https://dx.doi.org/10.1037/a0029063

Finkle, J. (2016, October 4). Johnson & Johnson warns public: Insulin pump is vulnerable to hacking [News]. Retrieved from http://medicine.news

Finnemore, M., & Hollis, D. B. (2016, July). Constructing norms for global cybersecurity [Academic]. Retrieved from https://www.asil.org/resources/american-journal-international-law

Fu, K., & Blum, J. (2014). Controlling for cybersecurity risks of medical device software. *Biomedical Instrumentation & Technology; Philadelphia, 48,* 38–41. https://dx.doi.org/10.11.1145/2508701

Fuentes, M. R. (2017). Cybercrime and other threats faced by the healthcare industry. TrendLabs. Retrieved from http://sillevis.com

Gardner, J. W. (2012). *Improving hospital quality and patient safety an examination of organizational culture and information systems* (PhD). The Ohio State University, Columbus, OH. Retrieved from UMI (3535103).

Gonsalves, A. (2013, June 14). Federal regulators address rising security risk to medical devices [Industry]. Retrieved from http://www.csoonline.com/article/2133604/network-security/federal-regulators-address-rising-security-risk-to-medical-devices.html

Grealish, G. (2016, June 20). The top 5 cybersecurity threats hospitals need to watch for [Industry]. Retrieved from http://www.beckershospitalreview.com

Hagen, S. A., & Richmond, P. (2008). *Evidence on the costs and benefits of health information technology* (p. 46). Washington, DC: Congress of the U.S., Congressional Budget Office. Retrieved from http://purl.access.gpo.gov/GPO/LPS94529

Halperin, D., Heydt-Benjamin, T. S., Fu, K., Kohno, T., & Maisel, W. H. (2008). Security and privacy for implantable medical devices. *IEEE Pervasive Computing, 7,* 30–39. https://dx.doi.org/10.1109/MPRV.2008.16

Harries, D., & Yellowlees, P. M. (2013). Cyberterrorism: Is the U.S. healthcare system safe? *Telemedicine Journal and E-Health: The Official Journal of the American Telemedicine Association, 19,* 61–66. https://dx.doi.org/10.1089/tmj.2012.0022

Harrington, S. E. (2010). U.S. health-care reform: The patient protection and affordable care act. *Journal of Risk and Insurance, 77,* 703–708. https://dx.doi.org/10.1111/j.1539-6975.2010.01371.x

Healthcare Security Alert. (2008, December). Healthcare's dirty little secret: Prevent staff members from snooping [Industry]. Retrieved from http://callisto10.ggimg.com/

HealthITSecurity. (2015, October 22). Breaking down the evolution of healthcare cybersecurity. Retrieved from http://healthitsecurity.com

HIPAA Journal. (2017, January 4). Largest healthcare data breaches of 2016 [Industry]. Retrieved from http://www.hipaajournal.com

Hisham, R., Ng, C. J., Liew, S. M., Hamzah, N., & Ho, G. J. (2016). Why is there variation in the practice of evidence-based medicine in primary care? A qualitative study. *BMJ Open; London, 6.* https://dx.doi.org/10.1136/bmjopen-2015-010565

Humer, C., & Finkle, J. (2014, September 24). Your medical record is worth more to hackers than your credit card. *Reuters.* New York, NY. Retrieved from http://www.reuters.com

Identity Theft Resource Center. (2017, January 19). Data breaches increase 40 percent in 2016 [Industry]. Retrieved from http://www.idtheftcenter.org

Information Systems Audit and Control Association (ISACA). (2017). State of cyber security 2017 [Industry]. Retrieved from https://www.isaca.org/

Jain, P., Gyanchandani, M., & Khare, N. (2016). Big data privacy: a technological perspective and review. *Journal of Big Data, 3.* https://dx.doi.org/10.1186/s40537-016-0059-y

Katz, J. J., & Fodor, J. A. (1963). The structure of a semantic theory. *Language, 39,* 170–210. https://dx.doi.org/10.2307/411200

Keyes, J. (2006). Knowledge management, business intelligence, and content management: the IT practitioner's guide. Boca Raton, FL: *Auerbach Publications.*

Knapp, K. J., & Ferrante, C. J. (2012). Policy awareness, enforcement and maintenance: Critical to information security effectiveness in organizations. *Journal of Management Policy and Practice, 13,* 66–80. Retrieved from http://www.na-businesspress.com

Koplan, J. P., & Fleming, D. W. (2000). Current and future public health challenges. *JAMA, 284,* 1696–1698. https://dx.doi.org/10.1001/jama.284.13.1696

Kusserow, R. P. (2013). Mergers and acquisitions due diligence in health care. *Journal of Health Care Compliance, 15,* 61–65. Retrieved from http://compliance.com

Lakhani, K. R., & Wolf, R. G. (2003). *Why hackers do what they do: Understanding motivation and effort in free/open source software projects* (SSRN Scholarly Paper No. ID 443040). Rochester, NY: *Social Science Research Network.* Retrieved from https://papers.ssrn.com

Landi, H. (2016, October 27). Report: The business of cybercrime in healthcare is growing [Industry]. Retrieved from https://www.healthcare-informatics.com

Lentz, C. (2010, December 23). How does refractive thinking relate to critical and creative thinking? | Blog: [Commercial]. Retrieved from http://www.dissertationpublishing.com

Levine, B. A. (2017). The cyberthreat to American healthcare in 2017. *Contemporary OB/GYN, 62,* 31–32. Retrieved from http://contemporaryobgyn.modernmedicine.com

Lord, R. (2017, March 15). Data security comparison: Healthcare vs. retail, finance, and government. HIS Talk. Retrieved from http://histalk2.com

McGlynn, E. A. (2008, April). Health care efficiency measures: Identification, categorization, and evaluation [Government]. Retrieved March 24, 2013, from http://www.ahrq.gov

Messmer, E. (2013, September 12). Medical identity theft on the rise. *CIO,* 2. Retrieved from http://www.cio.com

Miliard, M. (2015, December 3). Medical device security? Forget hackers, think "hand-washing." Retrieved from http://www.healthcareitnews.com

Modern Healthcare. (2017, January 21). Data points: Healthcare data breaches [Industry]. Retrieved from http://www.modernhealthcare.com

Myers, C., Powers, S., & Faissol, D. (2009, April). Taxonomies of cyber adversaries and attacks: A survey of incidents and approaches. *Lawrence Livermore National Laboratory.* Retrieved from https://e-reports-ext.llnl.gov

Nash, K., McGregor, I., & Prentice, M. (2011). Threat and defense as goal regulation: From implicit goal conflict to anxious uncertainty, reactive approach motivation, and ideological extremism. *Journal of Personality and Social Psychology: Personality Processes and Individual Differences, 101,* 1291–1301. https://dx.doi.org/10.1037/a0025944

Office of Disease Prevention and Health Promotion. (2014). Healthy people 2020. Retrieved from https://www.healthypeople.gov/

Papoutsi, C., Reed, J. E., Marston, C., Lewis, R., Majeed, A., & Bell, D. (2015). Patient and public views about the security and privacy of Electronic Health Records (EHRs) in the UK: results from a mixed methods study. *BMC*

Medical Informatics and Decision Making, 15. https://dx.doi.org/10.1186/s12911-015-0202-2

Perakslis, E. D. (2014). Cybersecurity in health care. *The New England Journal of Medicine; Boston, 371,* 395–397. https://dx.doi.org/10.1056/NEJMp1404358

Prater, V. S. (2014, December 8). Confidentiality, privacy and security of health information: Balancing interests [Acacemic]. Retrieved from http://healthinformatics.uic.edu

Pricewaterhouse Coopers LLP. (2013, November 15). Industry challenges facing healthcare providers, hospitals, academic medical centers, ACOs and doctors: PwC [Industry]. Retrieved from http://www.pwc.com

Ragan, S. (2009, May 8). Extortionist holds eight million health records for $10 million ransom [Journalist]. Retrieved from http://www.thetechherald.com

Rashid, F. Y. (2011, January 14). Data breaches at Arizona Medical Center makes case for zero trust security [Trade]. Retrieved from http://www.eweek.com

Ray, D. E., & Gallaher, D. (2015). Identifying and mitigating IT security risks in a merger or acquisition. Presented at the The Geek Week 2015 Conference, Atlanta, GA: ISACA Atlanta Chapter.

Reiss, S. (2004). Multifaceted nature of intrinsic motivation: The theory of 16 basic desires. *Review of General Psychology, 8,* 179–193. https://dx.doi.org/10.1037/1089-2680.8.3.179

Reuters. (2016, October 4). Hackers could in theory take over this insulin pump [Press]. Retrieved from http://www.nbcnews.com

Scott, W. R., Ruef, M., Mendel, P. J., & Caronna, C. A. (2000). *Institutional change and healthcare organizations: from professional dominance to managed care.* Chicago, IL: University of Chicago Press.

Shaw, E., Sachs, M., Parker, T., Devost, M. G., & Sachs, M. H. (2004). *Cyber adversary characterization: Auditing the hacker mind.* Rockland, MA: Elsevier Science.

Silow-Carroll, S., Edwards, J. N., & Rodin, D. (2012). *Using electronic health records to improve quality and efficiency: The experiences of leasing hospitals* (p. 40). New York, NY: The Commonwealth Fund. Retrieved from http://www.commonwealthfund.org

Socas, J. (2015, December 21). Growing pains: Cybercrime plagues the healthcare industry [Industry]. Retrieved from http://www.healthcareitnews.com

S&P Dow Jones. (2013). *Annual growth rates accelerate in January 2013: According to the S&P healthcare economic indices* (p. 4). New York, NY: The McGraw-Hill Companies. Retrieved from http://www.standardandpoors.com

Speaks, J. (2017). Theories of meaning. In E. N. Zalta (Ed.), *The Stanford Encyclopedia of Philosophy* (Spring 2017). Metaphysics Research Lab, Stanford University. Retrieved from https://plato.stanford.edu

Stolpe, M. (2016). The Internet of Things: Opportunities and challenges for distributed data analysis. *SIGKDD Explorer, 18,* 15–34. https://dx.doi.org/10.1145/2980765.2980768

Tafya, W. L. (2011, November). Cyber terror. Federal Bureau of Investigation. Retrieved from https://leb.fbi.gov

Thimbleby, H. (2017). Cybersecurity problems in a typical hospital. *Safety-Critical Systems Club.* Retrieved from http://www.harold.thimbleby.net

Tulasidas, S., Mackay, R., Hudson, C., & Balachandran, W. (2017). Security framework for managing data security within point of care tests. *Journal of Software Engineering and Applications, 10,* 174–193. https://dx.doi.org/10.4236/jsea.2017.102011

U.S. Congress. American recovery and reinvestment act of 2009, H.R.1 § (2009). Retrieved from http://www.gpo.gov

U.S. Congress. The patient protection and affordable care act, 3590 H.R. § (2010). Retrieved from http://www.gpo.gov

U.S. Department of Health & Human Services. (2017, April 26). Breaches affecting 500 or more individuals [Government]. Retrieved from https://ocrportal.hhs.gov/ocr

Vaas, L. (2016, February 26). Hospitals vulnerable to cyber-attacks on just about everything [Industry]. Retrieved from https://nakedsecurity.sophos.com

Wellington, K. B. (2014). Cyberattacks on medical devices and hospital networks: Legal gaps and regulatory solutions. *Santa Clara High Technology Law Journal, 30,* 139–198. Retrieved from http://digitalcommons.law.scu.edu

White Hat Security. (2017). What motivates today's hackers? [Industry]. Retrieved from https://www.whitehatsec.com

About the Author...

James C. Rice, MBA, DM/IST. Dr. Rice is the head of security consulting for Sirius Computer Solutions. He is responsible for aligning information technology services with strategic business objectives for clients. Sirius helps organizations solve complex business challenges so they can meet their business objectives. Sirius is an information technology consulting, sales, and services organization that provides best-of-breed business solutions for clients.

Dr. James is adjunct faculty with the University of Phoenix, School of Advanced Studies where he works with doctoral students. Dr. Rice is also a research fellow with the Center for Global Business Research. As a scholar, practitioner, and industry leader, he studies and writes about the relationship between information technology governance and the secure delivery of efficient digital business services.

You may follow Dr. James Rice on Twitter @DrJimRiceII or LinkedIn at /in/DrJimRice. To reach Dr. Rice for information on consulting or doctoral coaching, please e-mail: jim.rice@siriuscom.com

CHAPTER 7

The Cloud and Cybersecurity Threats for the Non-IT Leader

Dr. Susie Schild & Dr. Robert Boggs

Cyber threats are more commonplace than the public might think. Pick up any newspaper, watch any news program, and one reads about another data breach or cyber hack. Organizations need to give much more thought to where and how they store their proprietary, confidential, and private information. A non-information technology (IT) leader may wonder where the organization stores its data. Information is not only stored electronically on centralized systems in the company's server room, but company leaders choose to store offsite in many cases as well. Information may exist on electronic media, on distributed cloud storage, or in paper format. Individuals may also possess organizational information in different formats such as microfilm, microfiche, digital media, and other similar formats. An imperative is implementing robust physical security to restrict and control access of internal employees or external parties to locations where information resides to include the cloud. This chapter includes an investigation of the paradox of risks and benefits to cloud computing and traditional computing securities inadequacies for securing the cloud. Knowing only conventional technology practices threatens the security of cloud computing and presents an opportunity for refractive thinking.

In the early 1990s, convention limited electronic information mainly to systems inside an organization's four walls. As technology advanced, organizations sought less expensive data storage options and the volume of saved data skyrocketed. Years of digitizing data left organizations with data overload, ". . .of 520 executives surveyed from a variety of industries, 40% say data volumes are increasing in size and are becoming unmanageable" (Clemmons, 2008, p. 14). One example of how data becomes the victim of cyber threats and thus in need of a solution, comes from a security company, Recorded Future. In late 2016, a hacker breached the U.S. Electoral Assistance Commission (EAC) and then sold the access codes (Storm, 2017). Databases such as the EAC are likely targets as they store large quantities of user information that may be personally identifiable information (PII). Preventing unauthorized access in the early 1990s was rather simple, as one simply locked the door to the server room and access was limited to those with a need to know. Securing the cloud is not that simple.

The Cloud and Cybersecurity Threats for the Non-IT Leader

Problem Statement

Philippos Savvides, Technology Manager at EdPlus at Arizona State University (ASU), stated that there is a general misconception as far as people understanding what *the cloud* is (personal communication, April 4, 2017). People think information is just *up there* and not stored on a real hard drive. As people use the Internet and exchange information, information is transmitted and stored on servers, becoming vulnerable unless properly encrypted and stored. The cloud, where and how data is stored, and how to keep it safe are current priorities with University Technology Office (UTO) and frequent topics of discussion in UTO committee meetings at ASU (P. Savvides, personal communication, April 4, 2017). VMware software developer, Kevin Feshangchi stated,

> In my opinion, people really don't understand (the) cloud (personal communication, April 5, 2017). More vulnerabilities exist than people realize. We run programs that report thousands of risks to data every day. The layers of shared software and applications that have security flaws to begin with multiply in public cloud systems. (K. Feshangchi, personal communication, April 5, 2017)

Zhang, Raghunathan, and Jha (2014) supported Feshangchi, stating that current vulnerability issues in anti-malware programs are insufficient in combating continuously evolving malware attacks and vulnerabilities because of inevitable weaknesses present in today's highly complex software. Zhang et al. (2014) stated that weaknesses in anti-malware programs multiply for modern mobile devices, such as tablets and laptops using security methods designed for traditional desktops.

The general problem described by Abendan ll (2012) is that vulnerabilities are present in all software and operating systems. The general problem grows larger considering the findings in Celaya's (2015) study that identified organizations lack cybersecurity awareness. Layers of vulnerabilities combined with a lack of cybersecurity awareness present a problem. The specific problem this research addresses is that leaders, especially outside of IT, need a basic understanding of threats to cloud computing to guard against them and further the value proposition of cloud migration in their organizations. This research fills a gap in awareness and subject knowledge of threats to cloud computing for leaders in the following areas:

(a) defining cloud computing, (b) types of clouds computing, (c) use case, and (d) obstacles, benefits, and risks.

Defining Cloud Computing

Armbrust et al. (2010) offered the following comment regarding the understanding of cloud computing ". . . confusion remains about exactly what it is [cloud computing] and when it's useful" (p. 1). Hassan, Ried, and Hassan (2012) presented one way to understand the cloud; "cloud computing is simply the realization of the long-held dream of using computing resources in the same way as accessing public utilities" (p. 204). Understanding cloud computing requires a common definition. In this research, the definition for cloud computing is based on the definition provided by the National Initiative for Cybersecurity Careers and Studies (NICCS).

> (Cloud computing is) a model for enabling on-demand network access to a shared pool of configurable computing capabilities or resources (e.g., networks, servers, storage, applications, and services) that can be rapidly provisioned and released with minimal management effort or service provider interaction. Adapted from: CNSSI 4009, NIST SP 800-145. (National Initiative for Cybersecurity Careers and Studies [NICCS], 2017, para. 47)

The definition applied to an analogy of cloud computing is the vending machine example. Imagine the vending machine is the cloud. Resources are available in the vending machine. A user can buy options at the vending machine such as chips, soda, a sandwich, and four ice creams. These options are available whenever and as often as the user wants. The user pays only for the options they want (K. Feshangchi, personal communication, April 5, 2017).

Types of Cloud Computing

Types of cloud computing include a general description based on location or by the service offered. Based on location, a cloud can be private, public, or a hybrid (Čandrlić, 2013). Three basic cloud computing service models are *Infrastructure-as-a-Service* (IaaS), *Platform-as-a-Service* (PaaS), and *Software-as-a-Service* (SaaS). Service models define what the organization chooses to manage and what the service provider manages.

A **private** or **internal cloud** is a network used by only one organization or customer and is not available to the public (Armbrust et al., 2010). A private cloud at a remote location provides the highest cost benefit. Čandrlić (2013) pointed out that a customer may choose to house the network inside their own physical building and benefit from having physical control of the network.

A **public cloud** is when the whole network is located on the premises of a company offering a cloud computing service. The customer has no physical control over any of the cloud resources. Čandrlić (2013) explained that public clouds excel in performance as they use shared resources. Shared resources are most vulnerable to cyber-attacks, however.

A **hybrid cloud** uses private and public clouds, depending on their purpose (Čandrlić, 2013). High security risk data exist in a private cloud, while the less sensitive services and data stay in the public cloud. (Mathew & Nazar, 2016). An example is a store website. The part of a website the consumer sees is likely serviced on a public cloud because the public needs access to see the items they want to purchase. This information is not a security risk to PII, though hackers can still interrupt the experience of the public facing website. When a customer makes a purchase, personal data enters the system such as a credit card number. The personal data is housed on a private cloud, denying access to the public and thus keeping the PII secure. Three location based descriptions and the three basic service models help the reader build a framework of cloud computing.

Service Models of Cloud Computing

The number of service models continues to grow and become more specialized. Based on a service that the cloud offers, for the purposes of this research, this chapter refers to either: IaaS, PaaS, or SaaS. For our purposes, the need exists to break down the service models by what the organization should manage. As a baseline, we will use no cloud service. Figure 1 shows the areas of responsibility an organization assumes with each service model of cloud computing.

Figure 1: Cloud Service Models (reprinted with permission of Dr. Robert Boggs 2017)

IaaS refers to the type of cloud computing where a cloud provider *hosts* infrastructure components such as hardware, software, servers, storage, and provides access to them via the Internet. This type of model offers much flexibility if an organization needs to scale up (needs more service) or down (needs less service) quickly.

PaaS provides computing platforms, which are made of the hardware and operating system, and a set of components to complete a platform to run applications in the cloud without downloading or installing software on a local device (Mathew & Nazar, 2016). The user controls use and configuration of the applications, yet has no management oversight of the infrastructure (Mathew & Nazar, 2016). The transaction takes place on the Internet.

SaaS is a case where the user can access software provided and rents the software as a service rather than owning the software outright (Mathew & Nazar, 2016). Access is available whenever and wherever the user has a need. The user has the least amount of control over this cloud service. The provider rents access to both the resources, such as the hardware and the application. An example is what Microsoft Office is to the user. When using a SaaS cloud computing service, the user does not need to make a backup copy of the software; instead the design of the service supplies the software to all the users' devices through cloud (Mathew & Nazar, 2016). An example of how this service is useful is that in the event of three new employees, a company need only call its SaaS provider and ask to rent three more licenses of Microsoft Office, the morning of their arrival.

Understanding cloud computing models and services presents a need to understand why companies choose to migrate data to the cloud by investigating the case for cloud computing use and inherent risks. Refractive thinking moves away from old paradigms of data storage, usability of data, and traditional business-to-business relationships. In so doing, businesses contrive new ways to collaborate, compete, and innovate beyond what has been possible. A cloud computing use case informs readers about evolving practices and innovation that assist readers to begin the refractive thinking process.

Use Case

A use case for cloud computing is enhancing the collaboration between enterprises (Liu, Yang, Qu, & Liu, 2016). One use case example is effectively implementing cloud solutions through partner collaboration to enhance a company's competitive advantage (Truong, 2010). Demirkan and Delen (2013) suggested that cloud computing can support interorganizational business processes and workflow collaboration. Grant and Tan (2013) stated that cloud computing is the future for ultra-efficient support for interorganizational relationships.

Risks or vulnerabilities can happen at any level of cloud computing interaction. Though the use case in the paragraph above offers benefits, assume they all use Apple computers. In the first quarter of 2012, Apple announced the largest number of reported vulnerabilities and during the same period released an extensive number of patches (Abendan ll, 2012). Those vulnerabilities in the computer's operating system (OS) pose a risk to the safety of the data for all the users in the use case. A shared business process or workflow, in the use case above, accesses software in a public cloud. As complex software is impossible to produce without flaws, software vulnerabilities are unavoidable (Zhang et al., 2014). The number of threats, especially from malware, as reported by the Computer Security Institute, Symantec, and McAfee has exponentially increased since 2007. Various forms of malware include viruses, keyloggers, worms, botnets, Trojans, and rootkits, which quickly evolve and make defending against hackers and a host of threats a substantial challenge (Zhang et al., 2014). The challenge to data security is a layered and complex threat to overcome, yet companies engage the challenge for competitive advantage. A layered complex challenge requires a different framework of thinking and where refractive thinking is necessary.

Obstacles, Benefits, and Risks

Obstacles

Some institutions hold onto a mainframe system (yes companies still use mainframes, see an article by Davey Alba in WIRED Magazine from January 13, 2015) or client server and avoid some increased challenges to data security. Moving to cloud computing presents barriers and opportunities. Three main obstacles to cloud computing growth have been identified as: (a) adoption, (b) growth, and (c) business practices (Armbrust et al., 2010). Leaders may be slow to adopt new business practices because they are change averse or they have genuine fears that the various cloud providers may not have appropriate services for their organizations. Leaders may also be wary that the standard mechanism used to transfer data, *application programming interface*, is still fairly proprietary and unique to each of the cloud providers.

According to Armbrust et al. (2010), growth is the next obstacle organizations face. Organizations have valid concerns over how switching to cloud computing will affect their business. Some of those concerns may be: data transfer bottlenecks; reduced customer response time, and cloud storage scalability. Last, Armbrust et al. talked about business practices being an obstacle organizations must face. An example of a business practice would be a way to reduce risk to an organization's reputation should something negative happen with cloud service. Organizations must face contingency planning when something goes wrong. If an organization loses stored data or the organization's *eCommerce* platform goes down, the organization's reputation will suffer negatively.

Benefits

Though the obstacles presented may be a difficult landscape to navigate, companies continue to turn to cloud services in a big way as a measure to cut costs, and remain competitive. Armbrust et al. (2010) described that the benefits of large public cloud systems happen in situations when demand for technology services that could be managed in house varies with time and when demand cannot be determined in advance. Consider that the cost benefit of using 1,000 cloud computing machines for 1 hour costs as much as using a single machine for 1,000 hours (Armbrust et al., 2010). The 999 hours saved is a benefit. Further cost benefits point to minimization or elimination of up-front capital expenses that allows residual capital to be reallocated to other business investments (Armbrust et al., 2010).

Rapid evolution of cloud technologies adds more speed, power, and enhanced security to cloud platforms. These benefits cross industry segments such as vendors in the accounting market that also see benefits of scale (Needleman, 2017). A vendor with users working on the same version of an application incur lower support costs than the vendor that needs to support multiple software versions (Needleman, 2017). Cloud computing and storage remains very flexible for the customer and provider.

Risks

Flexibility has a price. Hacking into a computer's data or a cloud storage device is not difficult; hacking involves understanding programming language (Wilde, 2013). Hacking as a skill set is used to safeguard against cyber threats and to steal an organization's data. To minimize hacking risks, a company may not use the cloud. However, not turning to the cloud may render a company incapable of competing and the cost of continuing to privately host services becomes prohibitive. An opposing concern may be as IT departments downsize hardware, data centers, and staff, a point of no return exists where moving away from the cloud is not practical and reclaiming former institutionally managed computing capabilities is impossible (Barr, 2016). Additionally, consider the 2008 financial crisis and companies termed as *too big to fail,* and "the cost to our economy if a major cloud provider, like Google, Amazon, or Microsoft, were permitted to fail for any of the traditional business reasons" (Barr, 2016, para. 2). If a major cloud partner fails, companies will need a business continuity strategy.

Another risk consideration is the integrity of the cloud provider. Increasing numbers of functionality and features of cloud services, increased the risks for decision makers to choose a provider and ensure the procurement a trustworthy provider (Rajendran & Swamynathan, 2016). Organizations using cloud services need to have a high level of confidence in chosen cloud providers before they migrate their sensitive data to the cloud. As such, Rajendran and Swamynathan (2016) developed a model to calculate the trustworthiness of service providers as a means to determine reliability of service providers, to ensure that users can choose services with some assurance, and that the provider will not act with malice.

Commonplace in 2017 are reports by news outlets of

multiple hacking incidents that include examples of hundreds of thousands of customers' data stolen from breached government and school servers (Storm, 2017) and evidence of foreign governments influencing American politics by hacking into email servers (Williams, 2016). Security concerns are here to stay and will likely continue to increase.

Areas of security development are web application and malicious bot detection ("Continues Record," 2016). Botnets are groups of objects with unique Internet Protocol (IP) addresses controlled as a group, infected with malware and transfer data without the knowledge of the owner (Wired Staff, 2017). A botnet targets an online site and overwhelms the site with Internet traffic (Wired Staff, 2017). A 2016 example, called *Mirai,* attacked and temporarily disrupted individual websites, Internet Service Providers (ISPs), and Internet-backbone providers, which caused Internet access and service disruptions around the world. This kind of attack is a distributed denial of service attack (DDoS) (Wired Staff, 2017). As cloud computing service continues to grow, 2017 can expect more cyber-DDoS attacks.

In 2016, the Federal Bureau of Investigation (FBI) demanded Apple write software to decrypt its iPhone device so that law enforcement could access the data on an iPhone belonging to a terrorist (Wired Staff, 2017). This scenario again raised the question for user privacy rights. The conflict of encryption protection for users remains a continuing concern in 2017.

Security of data needs to be paramount in the decision-making process of IT leaders and organizational leaders equally. Top cloud service providers take security and the protection of customer data seriously, yet cyber-attacks still happen. Organizations should ensure adequate security measures are in place before access is granted to data.

Conclusion

Barr (2016) considered that as organizations continue to downsize IT staffing and reduce capital investments of hardware and data centers, organizations must consider the implications and reasonable limits of outsourcing data management. Information security risk continues to grow at an unparalleled pace, precluding a cybersecurity solution as a necessity for every organization ("ZENEDGE Continues Record," 2016). Understanding the increasing cybersecurity risks, knowing where an organization's data exists, and vetting the integrity of a cloud service provider remain growing concerns (Rajendran & Swamynathan, 2016). Barr (2016) stated concerns for data also include business continuity plans for data recovery or migration if a cloud service provider is suddenly unable to continue to provide service.

Despite the risks, advantages of cost savings and infrastructure development will continue to drive migration of data to cloud service providers. In 2017, growth for the cloud industry is an estimated 41% increase over 2015 (Butler, 2016) and investment in cloud infrastructure will increase speed, while cable networks expand (Hurbert & Etzkorn, 2017). These improvements will fuel enhancement of current services from cloud computing providers. Current cloud services include remote data centers that house multiple shared servers reducing capital investments for a business (Čandrlić, 2013). Needleman (2017) furthered the rationale for shared servers noting increased access to shared data, faster computing speeds, and the ability to quickly increase or decrease service. Such ability is representative of a just in time supply chain business model, but for a service.

The discussions leaders have across an organization about cloud services must be informed and knowledge based to bring value to the time sensitive and complex decisions that must be made. Cost benefit and security risks are a concern of every department in an organization, not just the IT department. A refractive thinking approach includes the multiple lenses of multiple leaders across the organization. Every department's leader has a goal, an intent, and a mission to move the needle toward innovation and increase profits in their businesses. The way in which innovation and profits are achieved are not always cohesive, easy to manage, or in strict alignment. The decisions that leaders make must continue to consider barriers, risks, concepts, benefits, future realities, and opportunities for refractive thinking for which this research provides a catalyst.

THOUGHTS FROM THE ACADEMIC ENTREPRENEUR

The problem to be solved:

Cybersecurity risks to cloud computing.

The goal:

- Raise the awareness of cyber risks and the need for security, thus increasing the non-IT leaders' value proposition in cloud migration discussions in their organizations.

The questions to ask:

- How can organizations effectively raise the awareness of cyber risks?
- How are organizational leaders outside of IT made aware of cyber risks?
- How technologically savvy are non-IT leaders?
- What is the level of involvement of non-IT leaders in the decisions to move their departments processes and information to the cloud?

Today's Business Application:

- Leaders need to recognize vulnerabilities in software and types of clouds to ward off cyber-attacks.
- Organizations are concerned with green technologies to reduce carbon emissions.
- Defending against mal-ware such as viruses, keyloggers, worms, botnets, Trojans, rootkits, and hackers increases data safety.
- Organizations find benefits of reduced costs, increased flexibility, scalability, and enhanced collaboration between enterprises.
- Businesses will look for means to encrypt data to ensure its security

REFERENCES

Armbrust, M., Fox, A., Griffith, R., Joseph, A.D., Katz, R., . . . Zaharia, M. (2010). A view of cloud computing. *Communications of the ACM. 53*(4), 50–58. doi:10.1145/1721654.1721672

O.C.A Abendan ll. (2012). *Gateways to infection: Exploiting software vulnerabilities.* Atlantic [Web log post]. Retrieved from https://www.trendmicro.com/

Butler, B. (2016, December, 19). *10 must-watch IaaS cloud trends for 2017* [Web log post]. Retrieved from http://www.networkworld.com/

Čandrlić, G. (2013, March 19). *Cloud computing-Types of clouds* [Web log post]. Retrieved from http://www.globaldots.de/cloud-computing-types-of-cloud/

Celaya, T. A. (2015). *Cloud-based computing and human resource management performance: A Delphi study* (Doctoral dissertation). Retrieved from ProQuest Dissertations & Theses Global. (UMI No. 10004286)

Demirkan, H., & Delen, D. (2013). Leveraging the capabilities of service-oriented decision support systems: Putting analytics and big data in cloud. *Decision Support Systems, 55,* 412–421. doi:10.1016/j.dss.2012.05.048

Grant, G., & Tan, F. B. (2013). Governing IT in inter-organizational relationships: Issues and future research. *European Journal of Information Systems, 22,* 493–497. doi:10.1057/ejis.2013.21

Hassan, Q. F., Riad, A. M., & Hassan, A.E. (2012). Understanding cloud computing. In H. Yang, & X. Liu (Eds.), *Software reuse in the emerging cloud computing era* (pp. 204–227). Hershey, PA: Information Science Reference, an Imprint of IGI Global. doi:10.4018/978-1-4666-0897-9.ch009

Barr, J. G. (2016). Cloud service delivery models & market leaders. *Faulkner Information Services.* Retrieved from http://www.faulkner.com.contentproxy.phoenix.edu/products/faccts/

Liu, S., Yang, Y., Qu, W. G., & Liu, Y. (2016). The business value of cloud computing: the partnering agility perspective, *Industrial Management & Data Systems, 116,* 1160–1177. doi: 10.1108/IMDS-09-2015-0376

National Initiative for Cybersecurity Careers and Studies (NICCS). (2017). *Glossary.* Retrieved from https://niccs.us-cert.gov/glossary#Z

Mathew, R. M., & Nazar, S. K. A. (2016). Cloud computing implication & exploration to green cloud: An overview. *International Journal of Computer Science and Information Security, 14,* 879–883.

Needleman, T. (2017). In the cloud today-and tomorrow: Online accounting is taking more and more of the market. *Accounting Today, 31*(1), 23–25.

Retrieved from https://www.accountingtoday.com/news/in-the-cloud-today-and-tomorrow?issue=00000159-468b-da34-a17d-f7cfea0d0000

Rajendran, V. V., & Swamynathan, S. (2016). Hybrid model for dynamic evaluation of trust in cloud services. *Wireless Networks, 22*, 1807–1818. doi:10.1007/s11276-015-1069-y

Storm, D. (2017, February 15). *Hacker breached 63 universities and government agencies* [Web log post]. Retrieved from http://www.computerworld.com/

Hurbert, S. & Etzkorn, H. (2017) The Atlantic: 2017 infrastructure analysis. *Submarine Telecoms Forum, 92*, 42–49. Retrieved from http://subtelforum.com/STF-92.pdf

Truong, D. (2010). How cloud computing enhances competitive advantages: A research model for small businesses. *The Business Review, Cambridge, (15)*1. Retrieved from https://www.researchgate.net/

Wilde, B. (2013, September, 25). *Hacking tutorials 101* [Web log post]. Retrieved from https://blog.udemy.com/hacking-tutorials/

Williams, K. B. (2016, December 16). *FBI, DHS release report on Russia hacking* [Web log post]. Retrieved from http://thehill.com/policy/national-security/312132-fbi-dhs-release-report-on-russia-hacking

Wired Staff. (2017, January 02). *The biggest security threats coming in 2017* [Web log post]. Retrieved from https://www.wired.com/2017/01/biggest-security-threats-coming-2017/

ZENEDGE continues record growth with key customer acquisitions. [Web log post]. (2016, November 29). Retrieved from https://www.zenedge.com/news/zenedge-continues-record-growth-with-key-customer-acquisitions

Zhang, M., Raghunathan, A., & Jha, N. K. (2014). A defense framework against malware and vulnerability exploits. *International Journal of Information Security, 13*, 439–452. doi:10.1007/s10207-014-0233-1

About the Authors...

Currently a resident of Arizona, Dr. Susie A. Schild holds several accredited degrees; a Bachelor of Arts (BA) from California State University Long Beach; a Master of Management (MM) from University of Phoenix; and a Doctorate of Education (Ed.D / ET) in Educational Leadership with a specialization in Educational Technology from the University of Phoenix School of Advanced Studies. She holds two Knowledge Management Certifications from Knowledge Management Professional Society, and is Lean Six Sigma green belt certified.

Dr. Schild enjoys hiking, biking, jet skiing, arboretums, and visiting local farms. Currently, she attends a women's technology group to learn trends in technology and have fun with HTML.

To reach Dr. Susie Schild for information on consulting or doctoral coaching, please e-mail: susanschild00@gmail.com

Dr. Robert Boggs resides in the Circle City of Corona, California. Dr. Robert holds several accredited degrees; a Bachelor of Arts (BA) in Economics with a minor in Geography from California State University, Long Beach; a Master of Science (MS) in Economic Policy and Planning from Northeastern University, Boston, Massachusetts; and a Doctorate of Education (Ed.D.) from the University of La Verne, La Verne, California.

Dr. Robert is adjunct faculty at the University of Phoenix, approved to teach business, economics, and management courses. He enjoys the interaction with students in the classroom and online helping them achieve their educational dreams. He also has held positions with DeVry University and Zenith Education Group as the Dean of Student Records and Assistant Vice President College Registrar respectively.

To reach Dr. Robert Boggs for information on consulting or doctoral coaching, please email: drboggs@gmail.com

CHAPTER 8

The Impacts of Integrity and Ethics on Cybersecurity in Higher Education

Dr. Temeaka Gray, Dr. Aaron Glassman, Dr. Cheryl Lentz & Dr. Gillian Silver

The evolving environment of digital technology presents many significant challenges to higher education. While advancements in the ability to connect to learning opportunities through distance bring much value—namely the ability to expand educational reach beyond traditionally served on-ground communities—the integration of virtual learning processes offers convenience and innovation that come with a cost, as well as unintended consequences. The focus of this chapter is to consider the impacts of digital technology on integrity and ethics within the post-secondary setting and how to manage this new platform for potential unethical behavior. The specific problem that requires attention is how educators must address the potential misuse of digital technology, namely the dilemma that accompanies more efficient access to information, and the temptation that then exists for work to be improperly attributed, copied from online sources, or even completed by someone other than the learner earning the degree.

Integrity and ethics, although often used interchangeably, are related concepts not entirely synonymous. Integrity, for the purposes of this discussion, refers to honesty, as underscored by Rhode (2006). Ethics refers to what is *right* in a given situation (Rhode, 2006). In line with this thought process, the question that arises when one can easily access significant volumes of content within seconds is whether those who avail themselves of digital technology do so with honesty and sufficient self-regulation. Is the contemporary student still completing their own work, devoid of shortcuts in sourcing and authorship? Or, are they leveraging technology to masquerade weaknesses in academic discipline? Some scholars in the literature suggest that compromises are increasingly common, as the temptation to fully exercise information volume and engage in ethical dishonesty is becoming more commonplace (Harbin & Humphrey, 2013; Michael & Williams, 2013). The refractive thinker, therefore, must consider the implications of cybersecurity in academia as the postsecondary education community gains a better understanding of the issues faced in this new digital age.

As first addressed by Silver and Lentz (2012) in *The Consumer Learner: Emerging Expectation of a Customer Service Mentality in Post-Secondary Education,* the American learner model is under dramatic transition. Challenged by time poverty and the need to manage lives at home and at work, the trend for the adult learner in the 21st century is to explore virtual learning options. In addition to removing the barriers of physical classroom-based access, distance learning allows students to engage in the assignments at any point convenient to them. The contact between the educator / facilitator and the student occurs through the learning management system (LMS), the telephone, e-mail, videoconferencing, and by text rather than face-to-face. The lack of direct contact may demonstrate itself in a certain impression of anonymity behind the screen—a factor which creates, in some, a less diligent allegiance to academic integrity. Certain practices, which could be repetitively discouraged or discussed at length in the physical classroom, may be conveyed primarily in policies and short reminders. A diffusion of responsibility exists. Although the faculty member may provide a stern warning within the physical classroom, the university becomes the messenger through the LMS in the online classroom, often far less stern in more friendly terms, often overlooked completely by the online student. The resultant message can differ dramatically leaving the individual student to willingly accept the accountabilities of monitoring their own ethical performance to avoid compromised choices in sourcing and assignment completion.

Teaching in the physical brick and mortar classroom offers an important distinction regarding the elements of cybersecurity in the digital space. As noted previously, when pursuing a degree within the synchronous in-person classroom, the student becomes well acquainted with the faculty member teaching the course, and a collaborative commitment can be cultivated. The faculty also gains insight into the individuals taking the course, while gaining a sense of their personality, and their accompanying performance strengths and weaknesses. Because of the regularity of the contact, and the capacity to provide real-time personalized feedback, there is no mystery for either side of the relationship. A psychological contract forms regarding student and faculty expectations, begging the question as to whether each side meets the needs of the other. The context of these discussions does change, however, in the online space in particular. The educator may know the name of the enrolled student, but no guarantee exists regarding ho really completes the work behind the screen (Silver & Lentz, 2012), unless institutions of higher learning invest in and require students to use certain technologies (e.g., multi-layer authentication, audio/video room capture, facial recognition, etc.) that have not widely been adopted. Many universities continue to experiment with hybrid variations that combine the convenience of technology (such as digital exams and in person labs), but under the close supervision of the in residence faculty. The potential of identity fraud compromises the student and faculty relationship; leading to fractured trust. The question of who really attends the course overall is uncertain, as the educator cannot confirm any suspicions they may have culled based on the quality of work patterns and to do so requires extensive documentation to university policies, as well as understanding of digital technologies. The larger question to contemplate is the responsibility of faculty regarding the detection of cheating.

The complication of understanding identity and personal learner commitment occurs more often in the digital space as both student and faculty attend the courses by logging in to asynchronous classroom environments within a digital LMS. The platform incorporates an e-mail address, a password, and perhaps security questions intended to verify and safeguard their identities to ensure authentication (Southern Association of Colleges and Schools Commission on Colleges [SACSCOC], 2012). The student log in regarding their indication of identity does not ensure the authenticity of the individual actually completing the work.

Faculty sign contracts with their respective institutions of higher learning agreeing to provide an ethical environment that supports, encourages, and facilitates student learning as dictated by the mission and value statements of the universities and colleges that employ them. Educators pledge to uphold the objectives and syllabi for courses. Further, they commit to build learner competencies to ensure that application and direct transfer into industry may occur (Silver & Lentz, 2012). The overarching intention is to enable the student to grow through their learning experience, and to benefit their industry and personal capacity for success as a result (Silver & Lentz, 2012). This model is incumbent on a genuine effort by the enrolled student, not a fraudulent unknown hired to complete the coursework on their behalf or the submission of work done by others. The educational relationship or contract between faculty and student requires a foundation that assumes integrity in effort, and the direct modeling of responsible judgment. The need exists for a proactive acceptance of personal and institutional ethical standards also is necessitated. The student assumes that the faculty name on their course is the actual faculty teaching the course; the faculty assumes that the student names on their roster are indeed the actual students submitting their assignments and posting their weekly discussion posts to fulfill attendance requirement. The question to ask is whether this scenario represents reality. What guarantees, if any, can the educator have of student accountability? How can the instructor discern the origin of the work submitted? How can original effort be distinguished from work too heavily shaped by pre-existing material, or authored by someone masquerading as the learner?

According to Kessler (2012), academia needs to "apply new ways of thinking, new understanding, and new strategies to the nation's response to cyberattacks" (p. x). This is where the concept of refractive thinking becomes especially relevant to the topic of student practice in the more remote but increasingly common world of online education. Despite the assumption that digital technology in and of itself already represents cutting edge and innovating thinking, the options for cheating increase exponentially as a result. Kessler and Ramsay (2013) suggested that "cybersecurity is about *process* rather than simply *technology*" (p.

x). Kessler and Ramsay indicated in their conclusions that a larger need exists for a multi-disciplinary approach for solution to include national defense, economics, sociology, political science, diplomacy, history, as well as the social sciences (Kessler & Ramsay, 2013, p. x). As a major enterprise within the nation that encourages cognitive growth and direct application to industry, thereby enhancing operational competitiveness, there are clear implications for academia when it comes to assessing and responding to, the imminent threat of cybersecurity and intentional misuse of the digital platform.

What Can be Done

Students feel pressured to succeed and faculty feel pressured to ensure the success of their process. As a result of these pressures, a major dilemma of cheating emerges and assumes new dimensions. Pullen, Orloff, Casey, and Payne (2000) referred to this problem as "the bane of higher education" (p. 616). Josen and Seely (2012) indicated that a "developing body of evidence that academic dishonesty is increasing with the increase in tuition the advance in technology and the increase in online class offerings, new ways to engage in academic dishonesty are available for potential cheaters" (as cited in Josien & Broderick, 2013, p. 94). Thus, *traditional* means that the educator and the institution no longer serve the traditional student nor do they support the traditional modality (Silver & Lentz, 2012). A new learner who consumes knowledge emerges, and sometimes, much like the shopper who purchases consumable goods, they seek others' support in completing the process (Silver & Lentz, 2012).

Faculty members perceived they are pushed toward

making students succeed because they are judged by their peers and administration at their respective colleges and universities, based on student outcome achievements. These benchmarks take the specific form of end-of-course completion levels, grade point averages, learning-outcome-attainment-data, and grade grievances. Student evaluations of faculty also come into play, especially for the adjunct faculty member, as they may not receive future course assignments at some universities if viewed by learners as too rigorous (Silver & Lentz, 2012). Little incentive exists, therefore, to move on suspicions of fraudulent activity behind the screen, as the burden of proof falls to the educator (Silver & Lentz, 2012). If faculty have the audacity to challenge the learner, suggesting the work reflects unusually high quality or is inconsistent with prior submissions, they may or may not receive administrative support. Subsequently, students are often left unaddressed to avoid false accusations or difficult to document concerns regarding student identity. Additionally, as underscored by Kessler and Ramsay (2013), faculty may become complacent in helping the learner to maintain their status, as challenges to the authenticity of their work may compromise their ability to obtain or maintain scholarships or competitive entry into professional programs.

The literature indicates that instructor concerns about student identity are genuine, and well-reasoned. According to Kidwell, Wozniak, and Laurel (2003), 74.5% of students are cheaters (as cited in Josien & Broderick, 2013, p. 94). The compromised behaviors typically take the form of student copying and compiling work that lacks specific student signature, purchasing a paper from the many available entities on the Internet with increasing sophistication and customization available to a specific course, and the latest trend is in student surrogacy—simply outsourcing going to class all together. One need only look to the popular website Craigslist for tutor postings that specifically state that the tutor will complete online courses, including research papers and exams, on behalf of the learner. In addition, a new breed of *homework help* websites has appeared. Sites like coursehero.com catalog student submissions by university, course, and activity and advertise themselves as study websites when in reality a student can download complete assignments for all course activities as submitted by other users. This website and others like them require the student to upload material before they are able to download material (or pay a fee) as a way of growing the website's repository of assignments making the website more attractive to future users.

The significant evidence of nonlegitimate student work presents a challenge to the instructor, and overall, the governance of by institutions of higher learning. According to Michael and Williams (2013), students employ recording, saving, and purchasing materials, taking tests in pairs or groups, and even paying someone else to enroll and complete course work for them as methods of academic dishonesty. The latter we have coined, *academic surrogacy*. The challenge becomes the sophistication from which students are finding these sources to either buy assignment completion or outsource attending class all together. Institutions of higher learning require proof of these sophisticated methods of cheating, challenging faculty who may not yet (a) be aware of such cheating schemes or (b) have the digital prowess or acumen within the world of cybersecurity to be able to catch a student and prove to administration such behavior took place in class. A foundation of understanding may be warranted to proceed forward.

Information security is a focus suggested by Kessler and Ramsay (2013), "refer(ing) to all aspects of security and protecting information from unauthorized access or use" (p. 37). This concept is relevant to college and university-level learning as technology access may be manipulated to intentionally create the appearance of original authorship or to infer work is being completed under the student's name. For example, a student can strip or alter the document properties of a document to make it appear as though they are the original author. In addition, The Homeland Security Act (2002) mandated that academia take an active role in homeland security education. Although this mandate does support the need for this chapter discussion, this emphasis remains concentrated on class content orientation and vague, focusing mainly on the physical sciences. The goal within this discussion is to shape the conversation at the beginning point of student enrollment and access to ensure authenticity of access in the classroom itself, as well as to the curriculum content. The importance is to take a closer look at risk vs. reward. "Risk assessment is also an important governance function, as it is essential that an organization's management understand the pertinent threats, vulnerabilities, and risk level of information in order to define the risk tolerance" (Kessler & Ramsay, 2013, p. 39).

It is no longer enough to simply buy answers for a midterm or final exam, students can buy previously submitted papers or newly created papers customized for their specific class, program, and university curriculum—-created just for them as the *consumer learner* (Silver & Lentz, 2012). Silver and Lentz (2012) created this term, the *consumer learner*, when discussing the challenges of shifting the paradigm of education from the concept of a *traditional student* to the one of a *consumer learner* in terms of shifting the concept of education—-particularly of the for-profit institutions—to one of customer service; the student is in the role of the consumer when they turn to the market place as a transactional exchange of trading money for buying student consumables such as discussion question posts, papers, and now hiring a surrogate student to attend class on their behalf all together. Despite the institutions requiring students to sign a student code of conduct or sign an ethical statement of intent, students seem more concerned with the *transaction* of the *business* of academia, with less concern with the opportunity for learning that academia was intended to represent (Silver & Lentz, 2012).

The Questions

Adding complexity to the dilemma of cheating is that students are often more proficient at using technology than the faculty teaching the course (Lange & Schultz, 2014). Educators must be aware of trends in academic technology and have a duty to prevent academic dishonesty to the fullest extent possible (Lange & Schultz, 2014). One of the impacts of this emerging digital educational paradigm shift is the continued expansion of *buying* the experience of an online education or candidly, the credential itself. Students find themselves short on time, but with the recognition of the importance employers place on college credentials (associates, bachelors, masters, and doctoral degrees) for career progression. Thus, the goal seems to be the pursuit of these credentials as a *consumer learner* (Silver & Lentz, 2012) to add to one's resume (business) or curriculum vitae (education) to include visibility in public social media platforms such as Linked In and Facebook, yet there seems to be less concern of the how a student attends school or what was actually learned—to include the latest strategy in student cheating: *outsourcing,* hiring a student surrogate to attend classes for them.

Dr. Temeaka Gray, Dr. Aaron Glassman, Dr. Cheryl Lentz & Dr. Gillian Silver

Surrogacy in the Academy: A Case Study

Universities are beginning to use similar methods as credit card companies to identify a surrogate user or an imposter or hacker—anyone other than the authorized user. However, unlike credit card companies that must defend against the use of stolen credentials, cheating within a university setting does not involve stolen credentials but a student who provides login credentials to a third party for the purposes of cheating. In this instance, the normal security precautions of a strong password, two-factor authentication (login + pin), etc. are all defeated with the sharing of one's login credentials. This sharing of credentials means the primary tool for identifying a surrogate user is through behavioral analytics and Internet Protocol (IP) address translation, a process that credit card companies use to detect unauthorized use (Dhanapal & Gayathiri, 2012). Each time a student makes a database call through a user click in the learning management systems (LMS) a single line of data is captured in a log file. This log line may look like:

27692, 54897, 862308, assignments/preview, 2016-11-21T03:41:16Z, 12.345.678.90

This data can be reidentified as Student ID# 27692, was inside class #54897, and clicked to preview assignment #862308 at 3:41:16Z on November 21, 2016 from IP address 12.345.678.90. The student, class, and assignment numbers can be easily converted to a student's username, a specific class (e.g., MATH 123), and a specific activity (e.g., Activity 1.2 – Module Discussion). In addition, the IP address can be translated to the name of the IP service provider, city, state, and other identifying information.

The following steps were used to best spot a surrogate user:

Step 1. Filter the log data so only ASSIGNMENT, SUBMISSION, and PREVIEW calls are present. This removes a substantial amount of irrelevant data from the data set; to prove a student is using a surrogate the university must show the surrogate "did the work for the student." Simply viewing the assignment or reading a content page does not rise to this level, so the focus is on assignments and submissions.

Step 2. Translate all of the IP address data to show city, state, country, and name of the IP service provider. This step can be automated using a programming language to parse the data set.

Step 3. Sort the data set by student ID number. This strategy allows one to review the data for patterns. Pattern discovery can also be automated using a programming language to detect certain behavioral patterns but can also be manually done depending on the size of the data set.

On the following page is an example of suspicious pattern worthy of further investigation (see Table 1).

Here one can clearly identify a surrogate user. A person with a Kenyan IP address previewed assignment #6790 at 8:08:08Z and then submitted the assignment a few seconds later. Then, approximately 4 hours later, someone in the United State previewed the same assignment. The pattern repeated itself the following day with assignment #6789.

Thus, it can be deduced that the student hired a surrogate in another country to complete the work and each time the surrogate informed the student the work was done, the student logged in to review the work of the surrogate. Although

TABLE 1. IP ADDRESS

Database call	Date/Time – Zulu	IP Address – City/State/Country
6789/submissions/previews	2016-11-21T09:25:56Z	United States – Providence, UT
6789/submission	2016-11-21T03:40:06Z	Kenya – Ebene
6789/submissions/previews	2016-11-21T03:40:08Z	Kenya – Ebene
6790/submissions/previews	2016-11-20T12:11:00Z	United States – Providence, UT
6790/submission	2016-11-20T08:08:22Z	Kenya – Ebene
6790/submissions/previews	2016-11-20T08:08:25Z	Kenya – Ebene

international examples are easier to identify, domestic examples can also be identified easily when comparing a student's normal login behavior with outlier login behavior. For example, one student hired a tutor at a different university to turn in work on their behalf. This submission was identified easily using the above behavioral analytics pattern matching schema. The argument exists that students travel, but the time between submissions is the indicator. It becomes highly unlikely that a student flew to Georgia to submit an assignment, flew home to California to preview it, and then back to Georgia to submit another assignment a few hours later. Although ways to fool these logs and spoof one's movements throughout the Internet, it would seem as though the vast majority of students using a surrogate would not possess those capabilities.

Universities continue to invest in remote proctor software, biometric verification, locked down browsers, and platforms that record audio / video of the student taking an exam that flag suspicious behavior. Although these technologies can and will prevent surrogacy, these strategies are not yet widely used and are cost prohibitive for many institutions. One must wonder if the reason universities are slow to adopt this technology is because they lacked the awareness of how wide spread this problem could be; something IP translation and behavioral analytics could better identify.

The Final Outcome:
Employer Concerns Post Graduation

The overarching concern and focus of this writing is the outcome of these impacts on integrity and ethics regarding the mastery of skills the student / employee / consumer will have when representing themselves to the business community for employment. Not only do academic institutions struggle with who actually attends school, but business owners will also struggle with hiring and recruitment of qualified individuals. The potential for identity and author fraud leaves the leadership of the enterprise wondering if the name on the resume represents the individual who attended the classes and completed the work, possibly making recruitment more difficult. The employer has no certainty that the candidate being interviewed is truly the person who completed the course work and academic training identified.

The Hiring Dilemma

One of the many impacts of these creative dishonesties is suggested by Josien and Broderick (2013). The authors placed emphasis on the practice that many firms engage in while on campus of requiring a minimum grade point average to sign up for interviews. Thus, for the unscrupulous or unconfident student, cheating to earn a higher GPA carries the advantage of preference. Students recognized that presenting higher scores correlates to their ability to advance in the business world after graduation. Literature indicated that younger, immature students cheat more than older, more mature students (Josien & Broderick, 2013). Upper division classes encounter less cheating than lower division classes, and unmarried students cheat more than married ones (Whitley 1998; McCabe & Trevnion, 1997; Park, 2003; Straw, 2002;, as cited in Josien & Broderick, 2013).

Students tend to cheat more at the end of their program, than at the beginning (Josien & Broderick, 2013). A related conclusion is that many seniors saw their colleagues cheat without consequences, and thus the option of *if you can't beat 'em join 'em* seems to be part of the emerging movement (Josien & Broderick, 2013). In addition, Josien and Broderick (2013) suggested that plagiarism is not as prevalent as in the past perhaps because of the *attention* paid to plagiarism and the integration of plagiarism detection tools in most learning management systems. Knowing that plagiarism will not be tolerated according to policy of the student code of conduct in institutions of higher learning is sometimes a preventative to compromised citation practice (Silver & Lentz, 2012). The emerging downside however, is that this caution in one area of conduct perhaps opens the door to more creative types of cheating, such as the idea of *surrogacy*—to simply cut out the middle man where the student simply hires someone to go to school for them.

Encourage Integrity and Ethical Accountability?

Students and faculty have a responsibility to academia and to each other. Students are responsible for their own education (Cook-Sather, & Luz, 2015). Faculty members include the responsibility for providing the opportunity for students to learn and for engaging student in a way that encourages learning. Engagement can seem elusive and tracking student learning in the online classroom can seem cumbersome and time consuming at a time when institutions of higher learning continue to ask faculty to take on more responsibilities in the form of additional teaching workload and committee work to meet the demands of tenure clocks. The question becomes, what is the incentive for spending the time and effort?

Ethics in academe is an important topic of discussion for faculty teaching in all levels of education and are a key component of the educational process. It is essential that faculty practice and teach ethical behavior (Turk & Vignjevic', 2016). Many theories about ethics exist and each one has a number of scholars willing to accept or deny their validity; however, it is important that some sort of consensus is reached *and* taught to students in a way that encourages students and faculty to remain ethical. Student handbooks ask that students follow specific rules with regards to academic dishonesty and detail what disciplines can occur when and if these rules are not followed. Contracts, appointments, and mission / vison statements guide ethical behaviors for faculty members. How are these ethical guides developed?

Ethical guidelines for faculty and students are based on ethical theories of what is considered *right* for society (Rhode, 2006). Leaders in government and organizations use concepts of universalism, utilitarianism, deontology, and consequentialism to construct definitions of acceptable behaviors for students and faculty; however, there is much debate over if one theory is best for all situations, or if more than one theory applies to specific situations. A goal of academic institutions, and therefor of faculty, is to be inclusive. Doesn't this imply, that sometimes the rules need adjustment to ensure that students are successful? So that tenure clocks do not run out? Why maintain integrity and why be ethical? Ethics serve many purposes, not least on the list is preserving the integrity of the educator's credential, preservation of individual reputation, and preservation of the reputation of the academic institution. Ethics remain based on what is morally right per society values. Dishonesty is not a moral right so any form of cheating in academia, including surrogacy must be wrong.

What We Could and Should Do

A goal of this chapter was to discuss the impact that digital technology has on academe and the need to contemplate the integrity of efforts invested by learners within their own educational process. Another goal of this chapter was to discuss what educators and students are responsible for in relation to integrity and ethics in academia using digital formats. Again, as digital technology uses computers to review resumes for key search words that match the job description and needs of the employer, how will the hiring authority have confidence that the applicant actually can do the job and truly possesses the actual skills as listed on their resume? How will society trust, but verify, skill mastery when looking to the newest graduates to join the corporate world to advance the world of business?

Ultimately, ethics are an important part of the education process. The key to avoiding unethical behaviors occurs in two steps; recognition and self-control. Students are responsible of exhibiting ethical behaviors despite the availability of technology that makes academic dishonesty easy. To achieve this result, students must make the conscious effort to recognize that the temptation to behave dishonestly exists, even for the *perfect* student. Faculty members are responsible for teaching and modeling ethical behaviors for the preservation of their credentials, to encourage ethical behaviors in their students to help them become ethical citizens of the world in a time when technological advances provide the opportunity to, and unscrupulous people and organizations encourage, achieve without paying attention to how achievements are made.

Conclusion

As presented in this article, the continually emerging world of digital technology offers many significant challenges to the world of higher education. Although digital technology offers the ability of education to expand its reach beyond traditionally served communities in traditional brick and mortar environments, offering convenience of the online classroom comes with a price. A question considered was whether the impacts on integrity and ethics within post-secondary education is worth the price paid. A truth discussed was that online learning is not a fad; it is an educational modality that requires educators to learn to manage a new era of unethical behavior in academia. As educators promise to uphold the objectives and syllabi for courses, they commit to build learner competencies to ensure that application and direct transfer into industry may occur (Silver & Lentz,

2012). The focus of this chapter was to explore the challenge to refractive thinking of the next generation of ethical dishonesty and cybersecurity faced in this new digital age to provide additional thought and purposeful discussion in thwarting this next generation of trying to circumvent the educational process.

Academic misconduct and integrity in postsecondary education is an international concern for stakeholders of postsecondary education (Chapman & Lindner, 2014). The impacts of the evolution of online education on integrity are vast, continually expanding, adding to the concern about integrity in the classroom. Traditionally, faculty faced the same issues of integrity violations regardless of modality. Documentation of student cheating whether on assignments or exams, fabricating information, facilitating academic dishonesty in others, and plagiarism are well documented (Erikkson & McGee, 2015). Issues of plagiarism (to include self-plagiarism) on assignments and exams are an issue seemingly as old as time. Not only do institutions of higher learning find and convict students of submitting papers by someone other than the student author, digital technology affords students the ability to buy papers by many disreputable businesses who will gladly sell students papers, problem sets, and discussion posts for specific classes, customized to meet their needs (Bain, 2015; Taylor 2014). The question of why should one do what is honest and considered right when there are in increasing number of ways and, maybe even, incentives to act dishonestly can be answered best by considering what are the cost and consequences to the stakeholders. Students have a duty to know what they say they know, educators have a duty to provide the instruction they say they have provided, and employers have an expectation that the employees they higher have the knowledge and skills they claim to possess.

THOUGHTS FROM THE ACADEMIC ENTREPRENEUR

The problems to be solved:

- How to identify and thwart new student cheating strategies within the digital space
- How to overcome the potential impact of cheating and student surrogacy on employer recruitment

The goal:

- Understanding how to prepare faculty to identify and prove various innovative strategies for cheating as well as student surrogacy.

The questions to ask:

- How can institutions of higher learning effectively prepare for student learning in the online space regarding the issues of plagiarism and student surrogacy?
- Can cheating issues be overcome to create strategies for managing student ethical behavior effectively?
- How will employers recruit quality candidates based on potentially incomplete or misrepresented educational achievements?

Today's Business Application:

- Institutions of higher learning need to create strategies to understand the student culture of cheating to respond successfully
- Effective administrative leaders within institutions of higher learning need to create effective identification strategies to understand the student culture of cheating to respond successfully
- Effective business owners need to create effective identification strategies of skill mastery regarding new hires

REFERENCES

Bain, L. Z. (2015). How students use technology to cheat and what faculty can do about it. *Information Systems Education Journal, 13*(5), 92. Retrieved from http://isedj.org/2015-13/n5/ISEDJv13n5p92.pdf

Chapman, D., & Lindner, S. (2014). Degrees of integrity: The threat of corruption in higher education. *Studies in Higher Education, 41*(2), 247–268, doi:10.1080/03075079.2014.927854

Cook-Sather, A., & Luz, A. (2015). Greater engagement in and responsibility for learning: What happens when students cross the threshold of student–faculty partnership? *Postsecondary Education Research & Development, 34*, 1097–1109. http://dx.doi.org/10.1080/07294360.2014.911263

Dhanapal, R., & Gayathiri, P. (2012). Credit card fraud detections: Using decision tree for tracing email and IP. *International Journal of Computer Science Issues (IJCSI), 9*, 406–412. doi:10.18535/Ijecs/v4i11.25

Eriksson, L., & McGee, T. R. (2015). Academic dishonesty amongst Australian criminal justice and policing university students: Individual and contextual factors. *International Journal for Educational Integrity, 11*(5). doi:10.1007/s40979-015-0005-3

Josien, L., & Broderick, B. (2013). Cheating in higher education: The case of multi-methods cheaters. *Academy of Educational Leadership Journal, 17*(3), 93–105. Retrieved from http://www.alliedacademies.org/academy-of-educational-leadership-journal/

Lange, T., & Towey Schulz, M. (2014). Higher education's role in academic integrity as it relates to technology. In T. Bastiaens (Ed.), *Proceedings of e-learn: World conference on e-learning in corporate, government, healthcare, and postsecondary education2014* (pp. 1084–1089). Chesapeake, VA: Association for the Advancement of Computing in Education (AACE). Retrieved from https://www.learntechlib.org/p/148883

Harbin, J. L., & Humphrey, P. (2013). Online cheating-the case of the emperor's clothing, elephant in the room, and the 800 lb. gorilla. *Journal of Academic and Business Ethics, 7*(1), 1. Retrieved from http://www.aabri.com/jabe.html

Homeland Security Act of 2002, Public Law No. 107–296, 6 US 188 &308 (2002).

Kessler, G. C. (2012, February). Information security: New threats or familiar problem? *IEEE Computer Magazine, 45*(2) 29–65. doi: 10.1109/MC.2011.262

Kessler, G. C., & Ramsay, J. (2013). Paradigms for cybersecurity education in a homeland security program. *Journal of Homeland Security Education, 2*, 35–44. Retrieved from http://www.journalhse.org/

Michael, T. B., & Williams, M. A. (2013). Student equity: Discouraging cheating in online courses. *Administrative Issues Journal: Education, Practice, and Research, 3*(2), n2. https://dx.doi.org/10.5929/2013.3.2.8

Moten Jr, J., Fitterer, A., Brazier, E., Leonard, J., & Brown, A. (2013). Examining online college cyber cheating methods and prevention measures. *Electronic Journal of E-learning, 11*(2), 139–146.

Pullen, R. Ortloff, V., Casey, S., & Payne, J. B. (2000). Analysis of academic misconduct using unobtrusive research: A study of discarded cheat sheets. *College Study Journal, 34*, 616.

Rhode, D. L. (Ed.). (2006). *Moral leadership: The theory and practice of power, judgment, and policy.* San Francisco, CA: Wiley & Sons.

Silver, G., & Lentz, C. (2012). *The consumer learner: Emerging expectations of a customer service mentality in post-secondary education.* Las Vegas, NV: Pensiero Press.

Southern Association of Colleges and Schools Commission on Colleges (SACSCOC). (2012). Resource manual for the principles of accreditation: Foundations of quality enhancement. Decatur, GA: Southern Association of Colleges and Schools Commission on Colleges.

Taylor, S. M. (2014). Term papers for hire: How to deter academic dishonesty. *The Education Digest, 80*(2), 52. Retrieved from http://circle.adventist.org/files/jae/en/jae201476033408.pdf

Turk, M., & Vignjevi?, B. (2016). Teachers' work ethic: Croatian students' perspective. *Foro de Educación, 14*, 489–514. http://dx.doi.org/10.14516/fde.2016.014.020.024

About the Authors...

Dr. Temeaka Gray resides in the mid-western town of Toledo, Ohio. Dr. Temeaka holds several accredited degrees; a Master of Business Administration (MBA) from Tiffin University; a Master of Nursing (MSN) from the University of Cincinnati; and a Doctorate in Psychology (Health and Wellness focus) from the University of the Rockies. Dr. Temeaka also holds an Online Teaching Certificate from the University of Toledo.

Dr. Temeaka, an Assistant Professor at The University of Toledo, teaches and works with students across undergraduate, graduate, and doctoral curriculums in the nursing program. She enjoys teaching and mentoring in psychological, sociological, and nursing disciplines. She is a member of the American Psychological Association, the Ohio Association of Advanced Practice Nurses, Sigma Theta Tau International (President elect of Zeta Theta Chapter at large, Order of the Eastern Star (Pride of Composite Chapter), and Delta Sigma Theta Sorority, Inc.

Dr. Temeaka is a Certified Nurse Practitioner at A Woman's Answer and owns Epiphany Consulting and Associates, LLC. She is the Chairperson of the Diversity Committee at the University of Toledo College of Nursing. She is a member of the University of Toledo Faculty Senate and Faculty Senate Executive Board. She has been recognized as an International Scholar by Sigma Theta Tau International Honor Society of Nursing. She is also a contributing writer to Nursetogether.com. Her doctoral study, *Exploring Stress and Stress Management in Managerial and Non-managerial Nurses,* afforded her the chance to gain professional and academic expertise to facilitate understanding within the healthcare community. Additional focused areas of research include communication and shared governance.

To reach Dr. Temeaka for information on consulting or doctoral coaching, please email: temeaka.gray@gmail.com. Her professional website is www.temeakagray.com

Dr. Aaron M. Glassman holds several accredited degrees; a Bachelor of Science (BS) in Human Development from Empire State College; a Master of Aeronautical Science degree (MAS) with a specialization in Human Factors, and a Doctor of Management Degree (DM) from the University of Maryland University College. He is also an FAA Safety Team Representative and serves on numerous panels, committees, and serves on the editorial review board of the Enterprise Architecture Body of Knowledge (EABOK).

Dr. Glassman is an Assistant Professor in the College of Business at Embry-Riddle Aeronautical University in the Technology Management department. His interest in cybersecurity and student surrogacy stem from a need to ensure degree authenticity and provide mechanisms from which to identify cheating. Using his experience in learning analytics, social analytics, forensic data analysis, and online learning, he believes that universities must actively safeguard against cheating to ensure degree value is preserved and industry can rely in degree presentation as a statement of personal accomplishment.

To reach Dr. Aaron Glassman for research collaboration, speaking opportunities, or consulting projects please email him at aaron@draaronglassman.com.

International best-selling author Dr. Cheryl A. Lentz, known as *The Academic Entrepreneur*, holds several accredited degrees; a Bachelor of Arts (BA) from University of Illinois, Urbana-Champaign; a Master of Science in International Relations (MSIR) from Troy University; and a Doctorate of Management (DM) in Organizational Leadership from the University of Phoenix School of Advanced Studies. She has her Sloan C Certification from Colorado State University–Global, as well as her Quality Matters Peer Reviewer (APP / PRC) Certification.

Dr. Cheryl, affectionately known as *Doc C* to her students, is a university professor on faculty with Embry-Riddle University, Grand Canyon University, University of Phoenix, The University of the Rockies, and Walden University. Dr. Cheryl serves as a dissertation mentor / chair and committee member. She is also a dissertation coach, offering expertise as a professional editor for APA style for graduate thesis and doctoral dissertations, as well as faculty journal publications and books.

Awards include: Walden Faculty of the Year, DBA Program, 2016, UOP community service award, and 17 writing awards.

Dr. Cheryl is also an active member of Alpha Sigma Alpha Sorority.

She is a prolific author with more than 32 publications known for her writings on *The Golden Palace Theory of Management* and refractive thinking. Additional published works include her dissertation: *Strategic Decision Making in Organizational Performance, Journey Outside the Golden Palace, The Consumer Learner, Technology That Tutors, Effective Study Skills, The Dissertation Toolbox,* International Best Seller: *The Expert Success Solution,* and contributions to the award winning series: *The Refractive Thinker®: Anthology of Doctoral Learners, Volumes I-XII.*

To reach Dr. Cheryl Lentz for information on refractive thinking, professional editing, or guest speaking, please visit her websites: www.DrCherylLentz.com, www.LentzLeadership.com or e-mail: drcheryllentz@gmail.com

Dr. Gillian Silver Rodis, ABC, is an accomplished 2 integrated marketing communications and strategic planning professional. Her extensive experience spans corporate-level vice president and director positions for companies with both domestic and international operations, and she has nearly two decades in the postsecondary education arena as a professor at the Bachelor's, Master's and Doctorate level.

Dr. Silver Rodis achieved a Ph.D. in Organizational Leadership, and authored the nation's first study on non-profit executive leadership. Further, she holds a Master's degree in Management/Organizational Development, and a Bachelor's in Mass Communications/Journalism.

Earning more than 200 writing, editing and project/campaign awards, Dr. Silver Rodis holds the prestigious Accredited Business Communicator designation from IABC. She was named IABC's "Communicator of the Year," NAWBO's "Woman of Distinction/Marketing," and is a Las Vegas

Chamber of Commerce's "Community Achievement/Communications" recipient. Further, she is an inaugural inductee into the Nevada Women's Chamber of Commerce Nevada Women's Hall of Fame. Dr. Silver-Rodis has been recognized for her competency and student-oriented philosophy with educator excellence awards from numerous organizations including the College of Southern Nevada, Maricopa Community College, and the University of Phoenix.

To reach Dr. Gillian Silver for information on, please contact her e-mail: GSilver@strategicresource.com

Index

B
Bitcoin, 20, 22, 55–56, 58–66, 68
Block chain, 62
Business continuity, 20, 30, 31, 133, 135

C
Cheating, 144–146, 148, 150, 151, 155, 157, 159
CPU, 76
Cognitive load, 159
Cloud-based computing, 4–6
Cloud technology, 4, 6, 9
Cloud, 20, 57, 123–135
Cryptocurrency, 55–58, 60–68
Cyber attack(s), 1, 2, 9, 19, 23–25, 27, 31–33, 64, 65, 76, 77, 80, 88, 89, 127, 134
Cyber crime, 30–32, 63, 102
Cybersecurity insurance, 32, 57
Cybersecurity workforce, 41, 46–48, 50

D
Data security, 1–3, 6, 7, 9, 10, 78, 131
Decentralization, 55, 60, 63, 65
Digital asset, 64

Digital cash, 59, 60

E
E-cash, 55, 58, 69, 68
Electronic data, 32
Ethics, 141, 154, 156–158

F
Firewall, 4, 27, 31

H
Hacker, 10, 22, 24, 26, 27, 31, 32, 63, 64, 75, 77, 80, 89, 99, 100, 101, 106, 108, 124, 128, 131, 151
Healthcare, 22, 25, 30, 76, 97–107, 110–112
Hiring, 1, 3, 7, 8, 39, 40, 42–46, 50, 111, 150, 154, 157
Human resources (HR), 1, 2, 7, 31, 45
Hybrid cloud, 127

I
Information security, 1, 2–5, 7–11, 19–21, 23–25, 28–30, 33, 39, 41, 75–77, 79, 83–89, 106, 114, 135, 148

Information systems security, 43
Information technology (IT), 1, 20, 21, 28, 41, 47, 76, 77, 85, 86–88, 123
Infrastructure-as-a-Service, 127
Integrity, 2, 11, 28, 41, 104, 133, 135, 141, 142, 145, 154, 156–159
Intrusion, 19, 24

M
Mining, 61

N
Network, 4, 5, 7, 10, 20, 21, 29, 31, 32, 47, 57, 60–62, 77, 78, 102, 106–108, 112, 126, 127, 129, 135

O
Organizational performance, 19, 20

P
Patches, 130
Peer-to-peer network, 61, 62
Phishing, 10, 22, 223, 27, 81, 111
Plagiarism, 155, 159
Platform-as-a-Service, 127
Privacy, 3, 5, 6, 11, 32, 58, 75, 76, 79–81, 83, 84, 88, 89, 99, 104, 110–112, 134
Private cloud, 127, 128
Public cloud, 125, 127, 130, 132

R
Risk(s), 5, 9, 11, 20–24, 28–30, 32, 33, 56–59, 62–66, 75–77, 79, 81, 85, 98, 101, 104–107, 110–112, 123–127, 129–136, 149

S
Safety, 10, 50, 59, 78, 97, 98, 100, 103, 104, 106, 107, 112, 130
Security awareness, 1, 3, 9, 10–11, 29, 88, 111, 125
Security breach, 23–26, 31, 59, 75, 77, 78, 97
Security threats, 21, 28, 107, 124
Server, 21, 62, 84, 123, 124, 126, 128, 131, 134, 135
Small business funding, 67
Social media, 150
Software-as-a-Service, 127
Student surrogacy, 147

T
Technology, 1–11, 20, 21, 25, 28, 32, 33, 88, 102, 104, 112, 123, 124, 132, 141–146, 149, 150, 154, 157–159
Telecommuter, 78, 80, 82–86
Telecommuting, 78–88
Threats, 8, 19, 20, 23, 28, 31, 41, 98, 107, 112, 123–125, 130, 131, 133, 149

V
Vulnerability, 2, 29, 30, 33, 50, 58, 78, 111, 125

The Refractive Thinker®
AND
Pensiero Press

2017 CATALOG

The Refractive Thinker®:
An Anthology of Higher Learning

The Refractive Thinker® Press

info@refractivethinker.com
www.RefractiveThinker.com
blog: www.DissertationPublishing.com

*Individual authors own the copyright to their individual materials. The Refractive Thinker® Press has each author's permission to reprint.

Books are available through The Refractive Thinker® Press at special discounts for bulk purchases for the purpose of sales promotion, seminar attendance, or educational purposes. Special volumes can be created for specific purposes and to organizational specifications. Orders placed on www.RefractiveThinker.com for students and military receive a 15% discount. Please contact us for further details.

Refractive Thinker® logo by Joey Root; The Refractive Thinker® Press logo design by Jacqueline Teng, cover design by Peri Poloni-Gabriel, Knockout Design (knockoutbooks.com), cover design & production by Gary A. Rosenberg (thebookcouple.com).

www.ThePensieroPress.com

I think therefore I am.
—Renee Descartes

I critically think to be.
I refractively think to change the world.

THANK YOU FOR JOINING US as we continue to celebrate the accomplishments of doctoral scholars affiliated with many phenomenal institutions of higher learning. The purpose of the anthology series is to share a glimpse into the scholarly works of participating authors on various subjects.

The Refractive Thinker® serves the tenets of leadership, which is not simply a concept outside of the self, but comes from within, defining our very essence; where the search to define leadership becomes our personal journey, not yet a finite destination.

The Refractive Thinker® is an intimate expression of who we are: the ability to think beyond the traditional boundaries of thinking and critical thinking. Instead of mere reflection and evaluation, one challenges the very boundaries of the constructs itself. If thinking is *inside* the box, and critical thinking is *outside* the box, we add the next step of refractive thinking, *beyond* the box. Perhaps the need exists to dissolve the box completely. The authors within these pages are on a mission to change the world. They are never satisfied or quite content with *what is* or asking *why*, instead these authors intentionally strive to push and test the limits to ask *why not*.

We look forward to your interest in discussing future opportunities. Let our collection of authors continue the journey initiated with Volume I, to which *The Refractive Thinker*® will serve as our guide to future volumes. Come join us in our quest to be refractive thinkers and add your wisdom to the collective. We look forward to your stories.

Please contact The Refractive Thinker® Press for information regarding these authors and the works contained within these pages. Perhaps you or your organization may be looking for an author's expertise to incorporate as part of your annual corporate meetings as a keynote or guest speaker(s), perhaps to offer individual, or group seminars or coaching, or require their expertise as consultants.

Join us on our continuing adventures of *The Refractive Thinker®* where we expand the discussion specifically begun in Volume I: Leadership; Volume II (Editions 1–3): Research Methodology; Volume III: Change Management; Volume IV: Ethics, Leadership, and Globalization; Volume V: Strategy in Innovation; Volume VI: Post-Secondary Education; Volume VII: Social Responsibility; Volume VIII: Effective Business Practices in Motivation & Communication; Volume IX: Effective Business Practices in Leadership & Emerging Technologies; Volume X: Effective Business Strategies for the Defense Industry Sector; and Volume XI: Women in Leadership. All our volumes are themed to explore the realm of strategic thought, creativity, and innovation.

Dr. Cheryl A. Lentz, managing editor of The Lentz Leadership Institute, explains the unique benefits of the books for readers:

"They celebrate the diffusion of innovative refractive thinking through the writings of these doctoral scholars as they dare to think differently in search of new applications and understandings of research. Unlike most academic books that merely define research, The Refractive Thinker® offers unique applications of research from the perspective of multiple authors—each offering a chapter based on their specific expertise."

THE REFRACTIVE THINKER® PRESS

The Refractive Thinker®: Volume I: An Anthology of Higher Learning

The Refractive Thinker®: Volume II, 1st through 3rd Editions: Research Methodology

The Refractive Thinker®: Volume III: Change Management

The Refractive Thinker®: Volume IV: Ethics, Leadership, and Globalization

The Refractive Thinker®: Volume V: Strategy in Innovation

The Refractive Thinker®: Volume VI: Post-Secondary Education

The Refractive Thinker®: Volume VII: Social Responsibility

The Refractive Thinker®: Volume VIII: Effective Business Practices for Motivation and Communication

The Refractive Thinker®: Volume IX: Effective Business Practices in Leadership & Emerging Technologies

The Refractive Thinker®: Volume X: Effective Business Strategies for the Defense Industry Sector

The Refractive Thinker®: Volume XI: Women in Leadership

The Refractive Thinker®: Volume XII: Cybersecurity in an Increasingly Insecure World

Refractive Thinker volumes are available in e-book, Kindle®, iPad®, Nook®, and Sony Reader™, as well as individual e-chapters by author.

COMING SOON!
The Refractive Thinker®: Volume XIII: Entrepreneurship

Telephone orders: Call us at 702.719.9214

Email Orders: orders@lentzleadership.com

Website orders: Please place orders through our website: www.RefractiveThinker.com

Coming Soon from *The Refractive Thinker*®
AVAILABLE THRU THE LENTZ LEADERSHIP INSTITUTE

The Refractive Thinker® *Volume XIII: Entrepreneurship: Growing the Future of Business*

Join contributing scholars as they discuss current research regarding the future of business regarding the influence of the entrepreneur. This volume will contain research shaping the conversation regarding what the future may hold to success of the economy in the hands of the emerging and evolving small business owner and entrepreneur.

COMING FALL 2017.

For more information, please visit our website: www.RefractiveThinker.com

Other Volumes of *The Refractive Thinker*®

*The Refractive Thinker®: Volume I:
An Anthology of Higher Learning*

The title of this book, *The Refractive Thinker®*, was chosen intentionally to highlight the ability of these doctoral scholars to bend thought, to converge its very essence on the ability to obliquely pass through the perspective of another. The goal is to ask and ponder the right questions; to dare to think differently, to find new applications within unique and cutting-edge dimensions, ultimately to lead where others may follow or to risk forging perhaps an entirely new path.

*The Refractive Thinker®: Volume II:
Research Methodology*

The authors within these pages are on a mission to change the world, never satisfied or quite content with what is or asking *why*, instead these authors intentionally strive to push and test the limits to ask *why not*. *The Refractive Thinker®* is an intimate expression of who we are—the ability to think beyond the traditional boundaries of thinking and critical thinking. Instead of mere reflection and evaluation, one challenges the very boundaries of the constructs itself.

For more information, please visit our website: www.RefractiveThinker.com

*The Refractive Thinker®: Volume II:
Research Methodology, 2nd Edition*

As in Volume I, the authors within these pages are on a mission to change the world, never satisfied or quite content with what is or asking *why*, instead these authors intentionally strive to push and test the limits to ask *why not*. *The Refractive Thinker®* is an intimate expression of who we are—the ability to think beyond the traditional boundaries of thinking and critical thinking. Instead of mere reflection and evaluation, one challenges the very boundaries of the constructs itself.

*Chosen as Finalist, Education/Academic category
The USA "Best Books 2011" Awards,
sponsored by USA Book News*

*The Refractive Thinker®: Volume II:
Research Methodology, 3rd Edition*

If thinking is inside the box, and critical thinking is outside the box, refractive thinking is beyond the box. The Refractive Thinker® series provides doctoral scholars with a collaborative opportunity to promote and publish their work in a peer reviewed publication. Our goal is to provide an affordable outlet for scholars that supports the tremendous need for dynamic dialogue and innovation while providing clout and recognition for each.

Winner in the 2013 Global Ebook "Non-Fiction Anthology" category; Finalist, the USA "Best Books 2013" Award; and eLit Bronze 2014 winner

For more information, please visit our website: www.RefractiveThinker.com

The Refractive Thinker®: Volume III: Change Management

This next offering in the series shares yet another glimpse into the scholarly works of these authors, specifically on the topic of change management. In addition to exploring various aspects of change management, the purpose of *The Refractive Thinker®* is also to serve the tenets of leadership. Leadership is not simply a concept outside of the self, but comes from within, defining our very essence; where the search to define leadership becomes our personal journey, not yet a finite destination.

The Refractive Thinker®: Volume IV: Ethics, Leadership, and Globalization

The purpose of this volume is to highlight the scholarly works of these authors on the topics of ethics, leadership, and concerns within the global landscape of business. Join us as we venture forward to showcase the authors of Volume IV, and continue to celebrate the accomplishments of these doctoral scholars affiliated with many phenomenal institutions of higher learning.

For more information, please visit our website: www.RefractiveThinker.com

The Refractive Thinker Press Wins 2011 eLit Award for Digital Publishing Excellence

The Refractive Thinker: Vol. V: Strategy in Innovation has been named the winner of the Gold in the Anthology category of the 2011 eLit Awards!

The Refractive Thinker®: Volume VI: Post-Secondary Education

Celebrate the diffusion of innovative refractive thinking through the writings of these doctoral scholars as they dare to think differently in search of new applications and understandings of post-secondary education. Unlike most academic books that merely define research, *The Refractive Thinker®* offers commentary regarding the state of post-secondary education from the perspective of multiple authors—each offering a chapter based on their specific expertise.

For more information, please visit our website: www.RefractiveThinker.com

The Refractive Thinker®:
Volume VII: Social Responsibility

The Refractive Thinker® Volume VII, is available to scholars and researchers. The book is part of the multiple award-winning REFRACTIVE THINKER® series published by The Refractive Thinker® Press.

Finalist in the "Anthologies: Non-Fiction" category of the 2013 International Book Awards!

Winner in the "Education/Academic" category, The USA Best Books 2012 Awards, sponsored by USA Book News

The Refractive Thinker®: Volume VIII: Effective Practices for Motivation and Communication

The Spring 2014 release of the Refractive Thinker® anthology marks a new direction for the publication. While previous editions have been curated from a purely academic standpoint, Volume VIII makes the real world connection by bridging the gap. Academicians identify and address the issues in each chapter and Dr. Cheryl Lentz, The Academic Entrepreneur™, provides an interpretation for application into today's business world.

This volume is a true bridge between scholarship and the business community.

Finalist in the 2014 USA Best Book Awards in the "Education/Academic" category.
2015 Next Generation Indie Book Awards Finalist

For more information, please visit our website: www.RefractiveThinker.com

The Refractive Thinker®: Volume IX:
Effective Business Practices
in Leadership & Emerging Technologies

The Refractive Thinker® Volume IX, is available to scholars and researchers. While previous editions have been curated from a purely academic standpoint, Volume IX continues building on the real world connection by bridging the gap. Academicians identify and address the issues in each chapter and provide an interpretation for application into today's business world.

Digital Only: $9.95. Under Business & Economics/Leadership publications.

The Refractive Thinker®: Volume X:
Effective Business Strategies
for the Defense Industry Sector

Join **General Ronald R. Fogleman** and contributing scholars as they discuss research regarding effective business strategies for the defense sector. The conversations include discussions regarding the struggles of a nation to define the way forward regarding the impacts of Defense procurement, Defense health care spending, economic impacts on veteran owned businesses and succession planning, solutions to manage and lead disasters, economic challenges, reduction of energy costs, and exploration of leadership strategies to drive business practices important to the future of our nation. The goal is this volume is to find innovative solutions for more effective outcomes to drive change.

For more information, please visit our website: www.RefractiveThinker.com

The Refractive Thinker®: Volume XI: Women in Leadership

Sally Helgesen and contributing scholars discuss research that will influence how women's leadership is understood and supported in the years ahead. They also offer fresh insights into mentoring and coaching practices, the impact of continued shifts in demographics, and the role of women in specific cultures in articulating a sustainable vision of the future. Such contributions will expand and enrich the programmatic offerings that help speed women on their leadership journeys into the future.

Digital Only: $9.95. Under Business & Economics/Leadership publications.

The Refractive Thinker®: Volume XII: Cybersecurity in an Increasingly Insecure World

Join contributing scholars as they discuss current research regarding the challenges of the world of cybersecurity and its effects in and on the marketplace. This volume contains research shaping the conversation regarding what the future may hold to protect businesses and consumers regarding the perils of digital technology.

For more information, please visit our website: www.RefractiveThinker.com

The Dissertation Toolbox

Struggling to complete your doctoral journey? Having trouble writing your dissertation or your doc study? Help is on the way! Join Dr. Cheryl Lentz—16-time award-winning author and Walden University Faculty of the Year in 2016—in her new book to help you shorten your time to graduation with proven and effective strategies. Save time and money learning to create systems to help move you forward through the process more quickly.

With Foreword by Dr. Julie Ducharme, Preface by Dr. Gillian Silver, and contributions from publishing intern Josue Villanueva.

www.ThePensieroPress.com

So You Think You Can Edit?
9 Self-Editing Tips for the Novice and Experienced Writer

So You Think You Can Edit? is Dr. Cheryl's most recent book that speaks to the precision of competent writing and editing. She underscores a myriad of practical techniques for validating our choices so we may refine our personal writing acumen, rather than relying on editors to carry the weight. Further, she makes a legitimate case for considering the impressions made when we speak through our articulation and review choices. Each of us, doctorate learner and business executive alike, stands to gain from her insightful guidance.

The Expert Success Solution
Chapter 5—What Would Einstein Do?

Join Dr. Cheryl as she offers proven strategies to shorten your learning curve to think beyond limits when facing problems in your personal and professional settings. Learn to fail faster to succeed sooner using proven skills to move you forward more effectively through individual coaching, Tele Seminars, and online classes using The WRIST Method. Remember, the helping hand you need is at the end of your W-R-I-S-T!

www.ThinkingBeyondLimits.com

The Unbounded Dimensions Series
by Dr. Stephen Hobbs and Dr. Cheryl Lentz

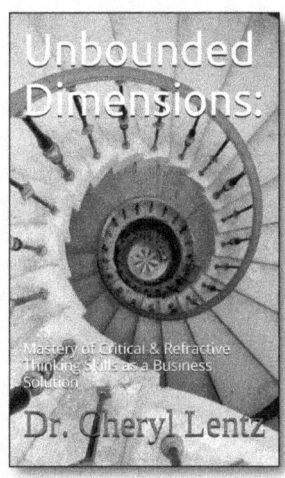

Unbounded Dimensions is a series of ideas, notions, suggestions, inklings, and guesses that the authors believe necessary to challenge mainstream management and leadership thinking and practice. These genius ideas are peripheral concepts and practices with grounded proof of working for the authors and their clients, yet lack mainstay researched exposure upon their presentation in the series. This developmental series enlarges these ideas for others to acknowledge, advance, and amplify in their workplace. In doing so, evidence-based research unfolds within workplaces to confirm or deny the usefulness, worth, and truth of the ideas.

www.UnboundedDimensions.com

Ethics, Employment Law, and Faith-Based Universities: When Law and Faith Collide

What happens when laws change in such a way that violate religious beliefs? This is a question that faith-based universities all over the country have been grappling with since the legalization of same-sex marriage in 2015. This paper attempts to give some guidance and direction to these institutions in applying discrimination laws and to open a dialogue about the ethical obligations to do so.

www.ThePensieroPress.com

PROVEN STUDY TECHNIQUES FROM
Pensiero Press

EFFECTIVE Study Skills
IN 5 SIMPLE STEPS

Dr. Cheryl Lentz has compiled the valuable information she gives in her blog in one easy-to-use handbook. The study tips are designed to help any student improve learning and understanding, and ultimately earn higher grades. The handbook is not so large that it requires long hours of reading, as is the case with many books on the subject. The information is written in a manner to help a learner "see" and "practice" proven study techniques. Effective study skills must be practiced to for improvement to occur.

www.ThePensieroPress.com

FROM THE LENTZ LEADERSHIP INSTITUTE

JOURNEY OUTSIDE THE GOLDEN PALACE
DR. CHERYL LENTZ

Come take a mythical journey with Henry from *The Village of Yore* and the many colorful characters of The Golden Palace on their quest to unlock the palatial gates of corporate Ivory Towers. This allegorical tale demonstrates the lessons learned when leaders in organizations fail to serve the needs of their stakeholders. Come join us in a journey toward understanding the elegant simplicity of effective leadership, unlocking the secrets to The Golden Palace Theory of Management along the way.

This revised second edition offers a companion workbook for discussion, reflection, and refractive thinking. Its purpose is to let the reader more closely examine each character and their leadership qualities. Take a leap of faith and follow us on our journey. Perhaps you may recognize some old friends on your travels.

www.ThePensieroPress.com

Pensiero Press PUBLISHES LANDMARK BOOK ON THE CHANGING ADULT EDUCATION ARENA

PENSIERO PRESS WINS FINALIST AWARD

May 12, 2012, Las Vegas, NV—*The Consumer Learner* has been named a Finalist in the Education/Academic category of the 2012 Next Generational Indie Book Awards and winner of the 2012 USA Best Book Awards!

Anyone who has entered a college classroom in the last 5 years has recognized a clear transformation in the context of higher education. A dynamic revolution in practice and delivery is underway, and the implications of change are ripe for analysis.

Administrators are increasingly charged with revenue production and institutional leadership. Faculty are experimenting with new models and advances in technology. Students are embracing new modalities as they strive to make curriculum immediately transferable into industry. *The Consumer Learner: Emergence and Expectations of a Customer Service Mentality in Post-Secondary Education* examines the new reality and emerging patterns shaping the experiences of these three diverse, yet interconnected, constituencies.

This book provides a distinctive approach to the transformation of the higher education culture within the U.S. Authors Dr. Gillian Silver and Dr. Cheryl Lentz, noted content experts, professors and curriculum/program developers, explain that the contents will initiate an intensive dialogue about the implications and impacts on administrative structure, faculty practice, and learner outcomes. Says Lentz, "This is a frank, encompassing work that has the capacity to ignite a national dialogue. We think the review will give voice to the significance of this evolving environment. The voices of experience leading this change will emerge."

Follow the authors on the Web:
www.consumerlearner.com

Available through Pensiero Press, a division of the The Lentz Leadership Institute. $24.95 (HARDCOVER)

TECHNOLOGY THAT TUTORS:
7 Ways to Save Time by Using the Blog as a Teaching Tool

University professors seem to have the same conversation with different students time after time. What if we could be available to our students whenever and wherever we're needed, virtually?

Technology offers such a solution with the creation of the blog. Think of it as technology that tutors 24/7. Welcome to the world of the blog where some of our efforts as professors are now scalable. Learn how you can create a video (with transcript), embed it on your blog, and simply provide the link to your students as the need or topic may arise in class discussions.

Please join me on this journey as I offer a path to shorten your learning curve with increased efficiency in teaching methods as we look to the blog with seven ways to save time by using the blog as a teaching tool.   Visit **www.TechnologyThatTutors.com**.

WELCOME HOME:
Siberian Husky Rescue Handbook
11 Tips to Welcome a Siberian Rescue into Your Family

Welcome to the Siberian Husky Rescue of New Mexico, Inc. Handbook for new Siberian owners.

Our goal for creating this book is to help new owners prepare themselves for welcoming their newest Siberian Husky rescue into their home. Making a decision to rescue can be one of the most rewarding decisions of a family IF everyone is well prepared. Proceeds benefit this 501c3 rescue group.

This book is written by Dr. Cheryl Lentz, the founder of Siberian Husky Rescue of New Mexico, International Best Selling Author, Speaker, and Professor.

Visit **www.DrCherylLentz.com/Siberian-Husky-Rescue**

PUBLICATIONS ORDER FORM

Please send the following books from The Refractive Thinker®:
- ❏ *Volume I: An Anthology of Higher Learning*
- ❏ *Volume II: Research Methodology*
- ❏ *Volume II: Research Methodology, 2nd Edition*
- ❏ *Volume II: Research Methodology, 3rd Edition*
- ❏ *Volume III: Change Management*
- ❏ *Volume IV: Ethics, Leadership, and Globalization*
- ❏ *Volume V: Strategy in Innovation*
- ❏ *Volume VI: Post-Secondary Education*
- ❏ *Volume VII: Social Responsibility*
- ❏ *Volume VIII: Effective Business Practices*
- ❏ *Volume IX: Effective Business Practices in Leadership & Emerging Technologies*
- ❏ *Volume X: Effective Business Strategies for the Defense Industry Sector*
- ❏ *Volume XI: Women in Leadership*
- ❏ *Volume XII: Cybersecurity*

Please contact the Refractive Thinker® Press for book prices, e-book prices, and shipping. Individual e-chapters available by author: $3.95 (plus applicable tax). www.RefractiveThinker.com

- ❏ *They Answered the Call*
- ❏ *So You Think You Can Edit?*
- ❏ *The Expert Success Solution*
- ❏ *The Unbounded Dimensions Series*
- ❏ *Ethics, Employment Law, and Faith-Based Universities*
- ❏ *Effective Study Skills in 5 Simple Steps*
- ❏ *Technology That Tutors*
- ❏ *Siberian Husky Rescue*
- ❏ *The Consumer Learner*
- ❏ *Journey Outside the Golden Palace*
- ❏ *The Dissertation Toolbox*

Please send more FREE information:
- ❏ Speaking engagements
- ❏ Educational seminars
- ❏ Consulting

Join our mailing list:

Name: _____

Address: _____

City: _____ State: _____ Zip: _____

Telephone: _____ Email: _____

Sales tax: NM Residents please add 7% gross receipts tax • *See our website for shipping rates.*

E-mail form to: **The Refractive Thinker® Press/Pensiero Press**
orders@lentzleadership.com

Participation in Future Volumes of The Refractive Thinker®

Yes, I would like to participate in:

❏ **Doctoral Volume**(s) for a specific university or organization:

Name: _____

Contact Person: _____

Telephone: _____ E-mail: _____

❏ **Specialized Volume**(s) Business or Themed:

Name: _____

Contact Person: _____

Telephone: _____ E-mail: _____

E-mail form to:

The Refractive Thinker® Press
orders@lentzleadership.com
www.RefractiveThinker.com

Join us on Twitter, LinkedIn, and Facebook

www.ingramcontent.com/pod-product-compliance
Lightning Source LLC
Chambersburg PA
CBHW070609300426
44113CB00010B/1463